The
Wisdom
of
Jesus

Publications International, Ltd.

Contributing writers:
Anne Broyles, Pamela T. Campbell, Theresa Cotter, A. Boyd Lutter, and
Larry James Peacock

Acknowledgments:
Page 19: Excerpts from *The Return of the Prodigal Son: A Story of
Homecoming* by Henri J. M. Nouwen, © 1992 by Henri J. M. Nouwen.
Used by permission of Doubleday, a division of Bantam Doubleday Dell
Publishing Group, Inc.

Page 85: Excerpt from *God Holds the Future* by David Meece and Brown
Bannister, © 1979 by Word Music. All rights reserved. Used by permission.

Page 114: Excerpt from *An Interrupted Life: The Diaries of Etty Hillesum*
by Etty Hillesum, © 1984 Random House, Inc. Used by permission of
Pantheon, a division of Random House, Inc., New York, NY.

All Scripture quotations are taken from the *New Revised Standard
Version Bible*, © 1989 National Council of the Churches of Christ in the
United States of America. Used by permission. All rights reserved.

ISBN-13: 978-1-4127-7901-2
ISBN-10: 1-4127-7901-4

Manufactured in U.S.A.

8 7 6 5 4 3 2 1

Contents

Blessed by His Wisdom

Something greater than Solomon is here!
Matthew 12:42

From the moment of his birth, Jesus made a dramatic impact on his surroundings. He was born in an obscure Jewish village about 2,000 years ago. Angels appeared to announce his birth, a bright star emerged to celebrate the occasion, and shepherds hurried to his humble cradle to honor the baby's arrival. Even the Wise Men from the East visited Judea to worship him when he was a toddler.

Jesus then grew up in Nazareth, and his quiet upbringing was punctuated by an important family visit to the temple when he was just a boy of 12. There, he amazed the teachers of the law with his uncanny wisdom and mature understanding of the ancient Hebrew Scriptures. The words and actions of their son, as well as God's unmistakable call upon his life, astonished Mary and Joseph.

Jesus, however, did not begin his ministry in earnest until he was about 30 years of age, leaving behind his vocation as a carpenter in Nazareth. Colorful and significant events marked the inauguration of his life as an itinerant preacher, much as his birth had been marked by such events.

John the Baptist announced his coming, and God opened up the heavens and poured out a blessing on his beloved Son.

For the next three years, accompanied by his small band of disciples and friends, Jesus traveled from place to place, preaching and healing wherever he went. Crowds thronged around him, eager to hear his wise words, his surprising teachings, and his memorable stories. Still others came for healing and encouragement.

From synagogue to seashore, Jesus proclaimed the good news of the kingdom of God, turning accepted social and religious ideas upside down. He pronounced blessings on the poor, he cherished children, and he treated women with dignity and respect. Jesus denounced false religion, hypocrisy, and sin. He called for repentance, and he promised joy, freedom, and new life.

Today, people look for grace and truth in his timeless words. It is our hope that you will be blessed by his insights presented in this book and by the inspiring thoughts of others about him.

When Jesus Asks You to Listen

Everyone then who hears these words of mine and acts on them will be like a wise man who built his house on rock.
Matthew 7:24

Action-Aimed Listening

To an increasing number of people, breaking certain "insignificant" laws doesn't matter. In fact, it may often look like the shrewd thing to do. After all, the police don't enforce the speed limit unless it's being exceeded by five or more miles per hour. Many schools don't dare enforce regulations on cheating unless it's an obvious major infraction, for fear of losing a costly lawsuit. Many businesses pursue discrepancies only so far because it is not worth the trouble, and from the bottom-line financial perspective, the cost comes nowhere near the relatively small return.

Breaking the Law

When you think about it, lawbreakers break down any society, little by little. Certainly that is obvious in the case of those who have a total disregard for law and government. That kind of outlook is called anarchy and, whether intended or not, will produce utter chaos.

Lawbreakers are definitely a destructive force in a society. If arrested for their crime, they may have to serve time in jail. And, if the offense is serious enough, they may lose some of their privileges as a citizen of their country. In that sense, lawbreakers are definitely the "least" citizens of a society.

There is also the factor of example with which to contend. Onlookers, especially younger people, often model their behavior after those they consider exciting and successful. Thus, "teaching" occurs through example, whether the lawbreaker realizes it or not.

Much the same is true in the spiritual realm. Those who break God's laws, even the seemingly "insignificant" ones, will be considered at the bottom of the ladder in God's kingdom. And the impact they are having on others' behavior will not be overlooked. The model of their behavior will be closely evaluated in the spiritual reckoning.

Obeying the Law

Sadly, law-abiding citizens in our country usually don't get the recognition they deserve. Because they do what they are supposed to do and quietly go about their business, they are generally overlooked.

Happily, that is not the case in God's kingdom. In the Lord's evaluation of what really matters for time and eternity, obedience to his standards and passing on that reverence to others is considered true greatness.

Isn't that refreshing and freeing to know? You don't have to be the best to be great in God's eyes. All it takes is an attitude of obedience to him and a willingness to model this attitude to others. If you do these things, no matter what your success in the eyes of the world, the Lord looks at you and says, "Great job!"

*　　*　　*

Dear Lord,

I have wanted to be great, but I didn't think I had what it takes. Forgive me for not realizing how you view greatness. Empower me to live out your gracious commands, and place before me the opportunities to tell others about true greatness in your eyes.

Amen

*　　*　　*

Holy Ears, Holy Words

In the clamor and noise of daily life, Jesus blesses us for listening to him with our hearts as well as our ears. The key to life is found in listening to Jesus in all the words and sounds around us.

A Gift from God

I find it helpful to remember that hearing comes
before speaking in a young child's development
of language skills. In our noisy, talkative culture,
we tend to overlook hearing as the foundation
of communication. We focus on words and how
to give them the proper spin, the right sound, the
persuasive punch. Yet, when Jesus commended
his disciples and showered them with blessings,
it's because they heard what people have longed
for throughout history. They heard the voice
of love.

Hearing is a treasured gift from God. When we
read the story of Helen Keller or see the movie
about her, *The Miracle Worker*, we are reminded
that we should not take hearing for granted.
Keller's deafness locked her out of the world of
meaning and relationship. I am always deeply
moved by the scene in the movie when Keller
learns that the water pouring over her hand can
be spelled in sign language. At age seven, she
finally begins to hear (and see) with her hands—
and the world opens up to her.

Our ears do open a world. They open the world of
sound and communication. I remember a retreat
leader urging us to put our hands on our ears
and to offer a prayer of thanks for our ears. Our
ears are always open. They bring the world to us.

Physically, we cannot shut them to the world. We are forever in the posture of openness. They are one of the pathways that God uses to communicate with us.

Listening Is a Skill

There's a difference between hearing and listening, however. We may hear words or sounds but not pay attention or seek to understand the message of the sound. Our ears may be open, but our hearts or minds may be closed to dealing with the information. My family has learned that when I am reading the newspaper, I am often absorbed in the story or events and probably will not hear what is said, even if I nod my head or say, "Uh huh." I have to look up and face the one talking to me so that I can fully be present to listen. My ears as well as my eyes need to be focused on the one doing the talking. Listening is a skill to be developed; it doesn't usually come naturally to most of us.

When Jesus addressed his disciples and blessed them for listening, it's because they understood the content of his message, and his message was that he had come to reveal the love of God for each person. At that point, the disciples had just returned from a mission and had seen the power of God healing and changing people's lives. Their eyes and ears were beginning to grasp the incredible, forgiving, renewing love of God.

We are invited to listen to Jesus, to hear the Good News. We listen by reading Scripture, slowly and meditatively, as if hearing and reading a love letter. We listen to Jesus through participation in a church community, listening to the hymns, songs, and prayers—spoken words that hint at the very presence of God.

We listen to Jesus when we listen to a friend speak of their sorrow or pain and we don't interrupt with our own aches or simple advice. We listen to Jesus when we get down on a child's level to hear about their trip to the zoo.

Listening Through Prayer

Perhaps the clearest way we can listen to Jesus is in prayer. We create the inner silence, the holy ground, where we can hear the still, small voice of God. Prayer is more than talking to God. It is also waiting for a word, a response, a nudge, a call.

As we develop the discipline of listening to Jesus, we will discover we are blessed. We will have our head cocked to the side and our ears tilted toward the sound of life. We will hear our own name called by God. We will begin to sense that we are God's beloved daughters and sons. We will know that we are forgiven and are made whole. We will touch our ears with gratitude and know deep in our hearts that we are truly blessed.

*　　*　　*

Holy God,

Give me an inner stillness, where the noise of the day is smoothed by the tides of your grace. Quiet my anxiety, hush my chatter, and give me enough silence that I may dwell in your healing presence. Give me a heart at rest and open to the sound of your voice. Speak to me of comfort or challenge, remembrance or renewal, and let me forever trust that you will lead me on the paths of truth.

Amen

*　　*　　*

God's Word Lasts Forever

The world has changed drastically since the time Jesus walked upon the earth. It's hard to conceive of Galilee 2,000 years ago. Yet, the humble man who spoke to shepherds, farmers, vineyard workers, and villagers continues to speak today to high-tech computer whizzes, CEOs of international corporations, politicians, and people like you and me.

The Voice of Jesus

How is it that words spoken to a particular people in a specific place long ago can still reach out to us? Why do the stories of Jesus transcend time and place to still find a ready audience in our hearts? What makes it possible for us who live in the early 21st century to understand the power of Jesus Christ?

Jesus was able to speak in images that his contemporaries easily understood: a shepherd looking for one lost sheep, a woman seeking her lost coin, a sower casting seed on the ground, and a vineyard owner hiring day laborers. Yet those stories make sense to us today, as well.

In our easy come, easy go world, we long for something permanent to cling to. We know that all living things die, all situations change, and nothing remains the same forever... except God's Word.

The words of Jesus beckon to us across the centuries, reminding us that God's love has been with us always and will surround us even after we leave this life and enter eternity.

The words of Jesus call forth our best listening skills. Christ's stories mean nothing if we don't make the leap from "That sounds good" to "What does this mean for me?"

His Words Are Timeless

Jesus' timeless words make sense no matter who we are. As we grow and change, Jesus speaks anew. So we bring ourselves fresh to Jesus' words, knowing that their timelessness will always have a word of relevance for us if we but listen.

Heaven and earth will pass away,
but my words will not pass away.
Luke 21:33

I Hear and Obey!

When I worked with a group of Girl Scouts on their God and Family Award, we talked about how often they squabbled with friends and how hard it was to make up. I told them about the conversation between Jesus and Peter when Peter asked about the number of times we need to forgive.

The girls gazed at me as I asked them to multiply 70 times 7. "490!" one child replied. "So that's how often we are to forgive other people," I explained. Silence. The girls looked at each other, appalled. Then one girl spoke up, "That's too hard. I think I'll just ignore that rule."

Most of us like to make our own choices and act as we wish. The Word of God gives clear guidelines for how we are to live. How can we reconcile our desire for freedom and God's desire to guide our lives?

Most of us have at least some rules we would rather ignore. Although Jesus gives us practical advice about living together, his words have little meaning until we put them into practice. Anyone can hear his words; it takes loving discipline to obey his commandments.

Trust and obey, for there's no other way to be happy in Jesus than to trust and obey.
John H. Sammis

What are some of Jesus' words that are hard for you to hear? Look at his words in Scripture. Then ask yourself, "What point was Jesus trying to make? Why have these words been difficult for me to hear? Am I at a point where I can make a new effort to give Jesus my loving obedience?"

Spend time in prayer with these questions. Then choose one area you feel ready to work on, so you might be one of the "blessed ... who hear the word of God and obey it."

* * *

Dear God,

I know that you care for me, and I know that you speak to me each day. I just have a hard time listening. I get so busy with my life that I often shut you out. Please forgive me. I want to listen to what you have to say to me. Help me be a better listener—most of all, a good listener to you.

Amen

* * *

When Jesus Asks You to Wait

Be patient, therefore, beloved, until the coming of the Lord. The farmer waits for the precious crop from the earth, being patient with it until it receives the early and the late rains.

James 5:7

Tested, but Not Testy!

When things are difficult for a long time, we begin to get impatient. Even if there is no apparent solution, we want to grab the bull by the horns and do something about it... anything!

When things are hard, we also tend to wonder if God is really there. It seems to us that this is the ideal time for God to intervene and do something spectacular. After all, that will prove he cares and is concerned, right?

You would have expected Jesus to reason that way. After all, he had been isolated and hungry on the back side of the Judean wilderness for weeks, all the while acting in service to God. At such a point of physical weakness, it would have been easy for him to impatiently expect his heavenly Father to provide miraculous protection.

But that wasn't the right way to handle things. Jesus knew that God provides and protects, without us having to force his hand to do so. Thus, Jesus, even in the midst of severe temptation, chose to actively trust that "Father knows best." That is one of life's most valuable lessons.

It is often said, "When the going gets tough, the tough get going!" But there should be a caution light. It is easy to go off unprepared and live to regret it later. How can you exercise patience in the midst of trial or temptation?

Doesn't it seem strange that we should not test God? After all, isn't he testing us on a continuous basis? Yes, but there is a big difference! The proper purpose of testing is to evaluate against the standard of perfection and to assess the need for improvement. Since God is perfect in every way, there is absolutely nothing to be gained by testing him. We, on the other hand, have a long way to go. Rarely is that seen more clearly than when we face trials or temptation.

✳   ✳   ✳

Dear Lord,
Forgive me for doubting you. I admit that I do not enjoy your testing me. But I thank you that the goal is to purify my life like spiritual gold.
Amen

✳   ✳   ✳

Compassion: Your True Vocation

The story of the prodigal son is one of the best-known and best-loved stories of the Bible. It has wonderful characters with whom we can identify: the rebellious and adventuresome younger son; the hard-working, resentful older brother; the caring, patient, loving father. It has plot twists and humor—who would have expected a good Jewish boy to be working at a pig farm? It has an unexpected and "feel-good" reconciliation, as well as the haunting question about whether the older son will join the party. It is a story we can hear again and again.

Though we focus on the prodigal son, the story told by Jesus calls us to become like the father, to grow in maturity and to develop a patient watchfulness and a compassionate heart.

This parable is known as being about a prodigal son, but it is equally a story about the patient and loving compassion of a father. The word *prodigal* means "recklessly wasteful or extravagant." In this story, we actually have a prodigal father who is extravagant and lavish with his love.

Be Like the Father

The late Henri Nouwen—Roman Catholic priest, author, and teacher—once wrote a book called

The Return of the Prodigal Son. He recounts how in his life he has identified mostly with the younger boy and sometimes with the older son. He was stuck identifying with those two until a friend said to him, "Whether you are the younger son or the elder son, you have to realize that you are called to become the father.... We need you to be a father who can claim for himself the authority of true compassion."

"You have been looking for friends all your life; you have been craving for affection ... you have been begging for attention, appreciation and affirmation left and right. The time has come to claim your true vocation—to be a father who can welcome his children home without asking them any questions and without wanting anything from them in return.... We need you to be a father who can claim for himself the authority of true compassion."

The Return of the Prodigal Son,

Henri J. M. Nouwen

As I have grown older, I see the wisdom in what Nouwen learned from his friend. Our true vocation lies in being men and women of compassion, who can feel another's pain and trust that in that solidarity a healing begins. I find myself less fascinated with the two sons and more drawn to the father.

People of Compassion

Sooner or later, it is the father who captures our attention, who draws us to a deeper place of being, who reveals our vocation as people of compassion. The father is patiently looking for the younger son. He is not anxious or fretting, but seems filled with a prayerful trust that God is watching over the wandering pilgrim. So he watches and waits, willing to let the young adventurer come to his senses. We do not know how long he waited, but he was ever watchful.

I want to develop such a patient vigilance in my life. I want that patient confidence as I watch my own children make their own journeys of discovery. I need a patient watchfulness because some things cannot be rushed but need the space and time to unfold. Such patient watching is ready, like the father in the parable, to respond with welcome and blessing, hugs and celebrations.

The father also looks with his heart, which is love. Compassion is not a technique mastered or a skill learned. Compassion is heartfelt solidarity with another. Compassion is an ache in the heart, a longing for another to find their true home.

There is a maturity in the father. He is not con-cerned about his own needs. His deep faith has ripened into patient compassion.

I am drawn to this mature compassion. I have been torn by labels: young/old, conservative/liberal, activist/contemplative. The father shows a compassionate heart. I want to move beyond separation and fear so that I can see everyone on the journey home.

Jesus tells the story to call us to his home from wherever we have wandered or from whatever resentments have constricted us. So abide in the compassionate love of God, which heals, forgives, and renews. Come home and learn to be a person of patient compassion.

So he set off and went to his father. But while he was still far off, his father saw him and was filled with compassion; he ran and put his arms around him and kissed him.

Luke 15:20

Rest for the Weary

The five-year-old boy exclaimed to his parents, "Man, am I stressed out!" His words seemed incongruous—how could a child be stressed out? The child was probably just repeating what he had often heard his parents and other adults say in anxious, frustrated voices. We don't have to read the headlines to know that our society moves at an extremely high speed. Many people are barely able to "keep it together," struggling to balance family, work, financial obligations, friendships, and personal time. There is much emphasis on time management. Increased use of computers and other high technology has led to an accelerated pace of life.

Jesus' Invitation

So how important is it for us to hear Jesus say, "Come to me, all you that are weary and are carrying heavy burdens, and I will give you rest"? Oh, we sigh, filling our lungs with deep breaths, someone understands! There is one who cares when our shoulders ache and our necks are tight with tension. There is one who listens to our inner heartaches and realizes our desire for peace. Jesus invites us to move closer to him, to lean against him, and to partake of his strength.

As a carpenter, Jesus surely knew how to fashion a yoke so that it fit the ox well and didn't hurt its neck. And as the Son of God, Jesus knows that each of us needs faith that fits us. We have enough burdens that cause anxiety attacks; the burden Jesus shares with us is not heavy but rather is a burden we can manage to carry. When we take Jesus on and put him into our lives, we will find rest for our souls. The stresses and strains of the world around us suddenly take on a new meaning.

All parts of our lives can be seen in the light of the love Jesus has for us. Yes, we may have problems with finances or relationships or jobs, but in the midst of all that is a God who loves us so much. Jesus came to share the load.

Jesus' Yoke

Take my yoke upon you, and learn from me;
for I am gentle and humble in heart, and
you will find rest for your souls. For my
yoke is easy, and my burden is light.

Matthew 11:29–30

Close your eyes and take some deep breaths. Feel the tension in your body. Imagine your to-do list with all the activities and decisions that weigh you down. Then picture Jesus coming toward you. As he nears, he places a yoke on your shoulders.

This is no ordinary yoke. This yoke is feather-light, made of love. Feel Jesus' yoke on your shoulders, and feel the tensions slipping away. Hear him speak your name and say, "Take my yoke upon you, and learn from me; for I am gentle and humble in heart, and you will find rest for your soul. For my yoke is easy, and my burden is light."

With all of the stresses and strains of our
daily lives, we need Jesus. His love makes life
bearable even when things are tough for us.

Give thanks for this gift and, when you are ready, open your eyes, knowing that the yoke of love that lies softly on your shoulders will help you face whatever stresses and strains are part of your life.

* * *

Gracious God,

Thank you for Jesus. Help me remember that he is part of my life at all times. He is there in the bad moments and the good, loving me no matter what happens. Sometimes I need a new perspective, God, because in the midst of all I do, I can forget that your love can carry me through. All the rest—the problems, the worries—are temporary, but your love in Jesus Christ is eternal. Let me take this yoke of love so that I might serve you always.

Amen

* * *

Justice Will Win Out

Sometimes it seems like the bad guys always win. Yet God promises that justice will win out in the end. How do we wait patiently until that time?

Occasionally, we read of a person who was wrongly imprisoned for a crime he did not commit. What did he think about, late at night, lying in his prison cell? Was he angry at those who gave false evidence against him? Bitter about the judge or jury who didn't believe his true story?

Resentful of the criminal justice system that, in his case, did injustice?

Consider this story in the Gospel of Luke:

[Jesus] said, "In a certain city there was a judge who neither feared God nor had respect for people. In that city there was a widow who kept coming to him and saying, 'Grant me justice against my opponent.' For a while he refused; but later he said to himself, 'Though I have no fear of God and no respect for anyone, yet because this widow keeps bothering me, I will grant her justice, so that she may not wear me out by continually coming.'"

Luke 18:2–5

The judge in this story doesn't care about God or the people he is supposed to serve. Justice does not seem to be a priority with him. We wouldn't want to be tried in his court!

Luckily, the judge is only half of the story. We also meet a persistent widow. We don't know the exact cause that she repeatedly brings to the judge. We only know that this widow is determined that justice will win out. In the end, the woman's efforts pay off and the judge relents.

Justice is truth in action.

Benjamin Disraeli

Jesus wants us to delve deeper into this story, to look at our own lives. Who am I more like—the judge or the widow? Of course, he wants us to be like the widow. He wants us to be persistent in our quest for justice, and if we are persistent, justice will ultimately win out.

Ready and Waiting

When I moved north to Illinois from Tennessee, I came with the same expectations and anticipation one might have in moving to the Arctic Circle. My suitcases were stuffed with boots, wool socks, a parka, mittens, and gloves. Packed away in my car trunk was a winter kit that included flares, a blanket, matches, 50 pounds of salt, and a flashlight.

And so, when Chicago had one of its worst winters, I was more prepared than most for the physical and psychological challenges of the snow that piled up and the wind chills that dropped lower than my outdoor thermometer could measure.

While I enjoyed building snowmen and creating snow angels, my neighbors complained constantly about what a fierce winter we were experiencing. The media reported on businesses that lost sales due to the weather. Everyone seemed distressed and unprepared but me!

Ten bridesmaids took their lamps and went to meet the bridegroom. Five of them were foolish, and five were wise. When the foolish took their lamps, they took no oil with them; but the wise took flasks of oil with their lamps. As the bridegroom was delayed, all of them became drowsy and slept.

Matthew 25:1–5

Sometimes we perceive those who plan ahead as dull and stodgy. I wonder how the foolish bridesmaids in Matthew 25 would have described the other five who dragged spare oil to a party! I'm guessing their comments were less than kind. Yet it is precisely this diligent preparation that grants us the freedom to be spontaneous and unconstrained.

I want to be just as prepared for future spiritual challenges as I was for my first winter in Chicago. I'll risk being described as a "religious freak" now if it means I'm prepared for Jesus' return. It's better than missing the party altogether!

✳ ✳ ✳

Dear God,

Grant me the patience to trust in your will and promises. Help me not to be overly anxious, but to be at peace, knowing that my life is in your hands.

Amen

✳ ✳ ✳

When Jesus Asks You to Trust

But if God so clothes the grass of the field, which is alive today and tomorrow is thrown into the oven, will he not much more clothe you—you of little faith?
Matthew 6:30

Even the Smallest Faith

When my children were very young, one of their favorite books was *The Little Engine That Could*. It was the story of a small train engine that admired all the big locomotive engines in the train yard but never was asked to do any significant work. I don't remember the reason, but one day it is asked to take a train of goodies for boys and girls up a big hill. The words it says as it huffs and puffs up the hill are, "I think I can, I think I can, I think I can." Over and over, the little engine repeats the chant until it succeeds in cresting the hill and then descends to a cheering crowd of boys and girls—with my children cheering, too.

What Is Faith?

"I think I can, I think I can" was one of the first notions of faith for my children. Size was not the important ingredient, but belief and desire. When my children first read the story of little David and the giant Goliath in the Bible, they learned again that size was not the key; it was David's belief that God was with him and his knowledge that he was very good with a slingshot.

Faith does not have to be grand, complete, big, or perfect. Faith is the willingness to believe, to trust that something can happen, so we give ourselves over to the effort. Faith for the Christian is the willingness to step out in confidence that there is a God. Faith is believing that God cares about us and is with us in all our efforts.

For truly I tell you, if you have faith the size of a mustard seed, you will say to this mountain, "Move from here to there," and it will move; and nothing will be impossible for you.
Matthew 17:20

With these words, Jesus encouraged his disciples to have faith, to trust a little deeper, and to have the confidence that with God all things are possible. He used two images that would be familiar to his listeners. Though mustard seeds are not the smallest seeds, it was common to use them as an illustration of smallness. Jesus encouraged his disciples' belief and confidence in this way. Keep trusting. Keep loving. Keep praying. You don't have to have it all figured out. Take one more step. Even a small step.

In Hebrew circles, great teachers would often use the image of moving mountains as a way of encouraging listeners to overcome difficulties. Jesus chose this second image, moving mountains, to point out to his disciples that the hardest tasks of life can be accomplished with the smallest amount of faith. What seems insurmountable and impossible, and as big as a mountain, can be overcome by even a little faith.

What Faith Can Do

I am deeply touched by all the things that happen because of one word or one act. Something that seems insignificant can make a huge difference. One visit to a worship service can start a person on the journey of faith. One teacher can make the difference for a student. One mountaintop experience or religious revival can call a person to a new vocation. One senseless tragedy can spur a community to open a teen center. One candle lit in the darkness can chase away the dark.

One afternoon, I mentioned to a church member that I wondered if she would be interested in creating a time and space at church where a storyteller could come to perform. She jumped at the idea and has birthed a program of bringing storytellers who attract new people to the church. One small idea met with the faith of one person, who then created the program.

In December 1955, Rosa Parks was tired from working all day and was glad for a seat on the bus going home. When some white people got on the bus, Rosa was asked to move to the back with the rest of the blacks. She refused, and her arrest motivated the blacks in Montgomery, Alabama, to call for a bus boycott. The person chosen to lead the boycott was a young pastor named Martin Luther King, Jr. One person's small act can catalyze a new "I think I can" movement for social change.

Believing and acting on your beliefs are important parts of faith. Jesus commends us for what seem like small acts or humble words. God transforms what we offer into hope for the world.

God can take our smallest acts, our seemingly insignificant words, and use them for good. We can turn our best efforts over to God and trust that they fit into God's plan for justice and peace, healing and unity upon the earth.

Faith Finds a Way

Conventional wisdom says, "Where there's a will, there's a way." But spiritual wisdom, the kind of wisdom that comes from Jesus, takes an extra, necessary step. Where there's a will, there's the ability to choose to trust. And where there's trust in the Lord, there's a way!

*Then some people came, bringing to him a
paralyzed man, carried by four of them. And
when they could not bring him to Jesus because
of the crowd, they removed the roof above him;
and after having dug through it, they let down
the mat on which the paralytic lay. When Jesus
saw their faith, he said to the paralytic,
"Son, your sins are forgiven."*
Mark 2:3–5

A classic example of faith can be seen in this
Scripture passage in which four people bring a
paralyzed man to Jesus to be healed. The crowd
that had come to see Jesus was so thick that the
people with the paralytic couldn't get into the
building where Jesus was. The huge crowd would
have been enough to convince most people to give
up and go home.

But these four were not most people. They firmly
believed Jesus could heal their paralyzed loved
one, and they were determined to find a way to get
him to Jesus.

Still, there was no way in through the conventional entrances. But why limit the options to
conventional ones? These people of faith decided
to go up the outside stairs and open a hole in the
flat tile or clay roof of the building. Through the
opening, they lowered down the paralytic directly
into the presence of Jesus.

Almost anyone else would have been shocked at the nerve of this plan to crash the party—right through the roof! Jesus, instead, was moved by the faith that motivated this extraordinarily creative approach. He did not scold the invaders. He commended them for their faith and extended the eternal gift of forgiveness.

Some people view obstacles as dead ends. Others conclude that those same obstacles are merely cleverly disguised opportunities. What makes the difference between these opposite outlooks?

Almost everyone encounters obstacles in their lives on a fairly consistent basis. The real question is, do you see them as insurmountable obstacles or challenging opportunities?

*   *   *

Dear Lord,

We know that if life were smooth sailing, there would be no need for faith. We thank you for the opportunity to trust you, in spite of the obstacles in our paths.

Amen

*   *   *

Be Worthy of God's Trust

When someone was needed to run a weekly tutoring program for elementary school children, Nicole applied for the volunteer position. She was only a high school junior and had never had this much responsibility, but she loved children and hoped one day to be a teacher. Nicole was thrilled to be given the job; she threw herself into her work, amazed that the school would trust her with the program. Nicole spent time getting to know the younger kids and their needs. She assessed the tutors, figuring out their strengths so she could team up young elementary school students needing help in math and reading with high school students who wanted to help.

> *Work is love made visible.*
> Kahlil Gibran

As she worked with the tutoring program, Nicole took on more responsibilities. She began to see herself as a teacher and found her own strengths in assessing learning needs and coordinating the program. When she received a community service award, Nicole was proud of what she had accomplished. In her acceptance speech, she noted, "As a teenager, it felt great to be trusted and then to be able to prove my trustworthiness. This experience has helped me know my own capabilities."

A Job Well Done

So [Jesus] said, "A nobleman went to a distant country to get royal power for himself and then return. He summoned ten of his slaves, and gave them ten pounds,

and said to them, 'Do business with these until I come back.'... When he returned, having received royal power, he ordered these slaves, to whom he had given the money, to be summoned so that he might find out what they had gained by trading. The first came forward and said, 'Lord, your pound has made ten more pounds.' He said to him, 'Well done, good slave! Because you have been trustworthy in a very small thing, take charge of ten cities.'"
Luke 19:12–13, 15–17

Nicole realized what the slave in this parable discovered when his master gave him one pound to use, instructed only to "Do business with [this] until I come back." The first slave was able to come forward when the nobleman returned and say, "Lord, your pound has made ten more pounds." It pleased the master to know that this slave had made good use of his money, so he rewarded the slave with more responsibility "because you have been trustworthy in a very small thing."

God gives us life and trusts that we will live it well and wisely. If we use the gifts God has given us, we will be rewarded and see positive results for our efforts.

It feels great to earn another's trust. When someone gives us a job, assumes we can handle the tasks at hand, or wants our input, we get the message: We are valued. God, in giving us not only our very lives but the freedom to make our own choices, trusts our spirits as well as our capabilities.

A Trustworthy Life

Look at your life. How have you proved trust-worthy to God? What actions have you taken that best respond to a loving Creator who wants to count on you as a faithful servant? Have you felt rewarded for a life well lived? Hear God say to you, "Well done!"

I am no longer my own, but thine. Put me to what thou wilt, rank me with whom thou wilt... Let me be full, let me be empty. Let me have all things, let me have nothing. I freely and heartily yield all things to thy pleasure and disposal... thou art mine, and I am thine...
John Wesley

This is an important time to also admit the in-stances when you may not have fulfilled God's expectations. Were you more like the other slave (see Luke 19:20–22) who did nothing with the money, fearing what the master might do? Do you have gifts and talents you have been reluctant to use for God's service? Let this parable open a door in your heart so that you might be bold in living a trustworthy life.

Water, Wind, and Faith

*A windstorm arose on the sea, so great that
the boat was being swamped by the waves; but
he was asleep. And they went and woke him up,
saying, "Lord, save us! We are perishing!" And he
said to them, "Why are you afraid, you of little
faith?" Then he got up and rebuked the winds
and the sea; and there was a dead calm.*
Matthew 8:24–26

Even when there is no water around, we know
what it is like to be in that boat. We even use
similar language. We have "stormy" days, "stormy"
relationships. We are "swamped" by all the work
we have to do. We feel the list growing of things
to do. We see the approaching deadlines. We
know the pressure to achieve much and accom-
plish more. When we add the family calendar, the
relatives, and the needs of the world, our boat
often seems ready to capsize.

*Jesus challenges us to have faith in God even
in the midst of the windstorms of our lives.*

Sometimes it feels like there is no way out. The
problems threaten to dump us into the sea, and
we cannot see how we are going to make it. At
such times we cry out, "Help!" We want Jesus,
or someone, to save us. Scripture is full of such
cries. "Save me, O God, for the waters have come
up to my neck" (Psalm 69:1).

At its core, faith is not a system of knowledge, but trust.
Joseph Ratzinger

We are in good company when we cry out to God. Our challenge is to trust that not only does God hear our cry, but he is also working in the very midst of our windstorm. Jesus is revealing to the disciples and to us a God who cares for the well-being of all people, especially those feeling swamped. We need not worry how God will calm the storms, only that he will. Each storm calmed leads us to greater trust, a deeper faith. God can help us deal with the constant pressures of our days. God can bring calm to our stormy lives.

Facing the Storm

[Jesus] woke up and rebuked the wind, and said to the sea, "Peace! Be still!" Then the wind ceased, and there was a dead calm. He said to [his disciples], "Why are you afraid? Have you still no faith?" And they were filled with great awe and said to one another, "Who then is this, that even the wind and the sea obey him?"
Mark 4:39–41

Jesus was asleep when the storm began. As the wind stirred up the waves on the Sea of Galilee, the others became more and more afraid, realizing that this voyage could be their last if the boat capsized or sank.

Terrified, they awoke their teacher. He rebuked
the storm and the wind ceased, leaving only the
shining calm of the lake's surface under and
around the boat. Jesus must have seen something
on his followers' faces that showed that their
fear was not assuaged. "Why are you afraid?" he
asked. "Have you still no faith?" It was then that
the truth sank in: Jesus had calmed the storm.
"Who then is this," they cried, "that even the wind
and the sea obey him?"

All along, there had been some who followed
Jesus only to see the miracles. He may have been
for them a worker of magic, the best show in
town. They may have been attracted by his story-
telling, intrigued by his teachings. Now his power
had been revealed. This was no sideshow magi-
cian; he could calm storms.

*Whatever storms we face, Jesus has the
power to calm our fears if we recognize him
and allow him to take charge of our lives.*

Perhaps it was then that all Jesus had ever said
began to make sense. Now, on a boat out at sea,
some of Jesus' followers realized that this powerful man was one to whom they could commit
their lives. Little did they know that 2,000 years
later, Jesus would still be calming the fears and
stormy lives of his followers.

*　　*　　*

Loving Jesus,

We need you. Our boat is small and the sea is large, and we are sometimes afraid. Be with us as we remember that in you is our salvation.

Amen

*　　*　　*

An Invitation to Believe

When I was in high school, I played doubles on the tennis team. It was a lesson in trust and faith, as well as a lot of fun. I had to have faith that my partner would get to the balls that were hit on his side of the court and that he would be able to win his serve or get the next point (especially if I had just made an error). This faith was based on experience, on past games when he had come through. This faith enabled me to do my part and not run on his side of the court whenever a ball was hit to him. Faith in my partner and faith in myself led to a successful way of playing. Indeed, it was a commitment based on faith.

Faith Is a Way of Living

[Jesus] answered them, "You faithless generation, how much longer must I be among you? How much longer must I put up with you? Bring him to me." And they brought the boy to him. When the

spirit saw him, immediately it convulsed the boy...
Jesus asked the father, "How long has this been
happening to him?" And he said, "From childhood.
It has often cast him into the fire and into the water,
to destroy him; but if you are able to do anything,
have pity on us and help us." Jesus said to him, "If
you are able!—All things can be done for the one
who believes." Immediately the father of the child
cried out, "I believe; help my unbelief!"
Mark 9:19–24

Jesus lamented the lack of faith in his disciples,
the crowd, and even the father. Such a lack of
faith is paralyzing, and when Jesus arrived on the
scene, he learned that the disciples could not help
the boy. A whole world of disbelief dwelt in that
crowd and stood in the way of healing.

Our generation may not be much different; we too
often doubt the power of God to work in our contemporary situations. Sometimes we feel that the
international problems, the violence in cities, and
the growing numbers of the homeless are beyond
the realm of solutions. We often don't believe that
God can figure out how to solve the mess we have
gotten ourselves into.

Jesus knows how hard it is to have faith in these
trying times. We are a mixture of belief and unbelief. We believe there is a God, yet we are timid
in believing that God can bring about healing or

world peace. We see evidence of God in the wonders of creation, yet we find it difficult to see how God is at work in our hurt and pain. Jesus wants us to deepen our trust in God. He wants us to come to God sooner with our requests and needs. He wants us to know that God desires to help us and is able to help us.

> *Jesus wants to move us from unbelief to belief. He invites us to trust God, beginning with the simple, ordinary moments of life.*

Such faith is a gift. We do not earn God's help. It is offered before we are even aware that we have needs. We simply turn and receive. We "let go and let God." Faith is not some system of knowledge that we have to master, but rather it is a way of trusting. Faith is not a set of propositions to believe but a way of living with what small measure of confidence in God that we have. We start small, perhaps thanking God for the gift of a new day. We look around at creation and let a prayer of thanks arise. Start with one rose, one sunrise, and say, "Thank you."

A Faith That Grows

A friend of mine came to church one Sunday to help honor the nursery school teachers who taught his children. He had missed the services we had done previous years, but on this Sunday, he decided to come. He says he felt so safe in the sanctuary that he cried through much of the service. The tears were the beginning of his faith. It was a small thing, to come to church, and he did not understand what the tears meant, but it was the beginning of turning himself over to God. He has hardly missed a Sunday since, and he soon started coming to some classes and dropping by the office during the week. Each day, he was learning to trust God more. The day of his baptism was a glorious day, and he is daily moving from unbelief to belief.

> *Faith is a firm and certain knowledge*
> *of God's benevolence toward us, founded upon*
> *the truth of the freely given promise in Christ,*
> *both revealed to our minds and sealed upon*
> *our hearts through the Holy Spirit.*
> John Calvin

We learn over and over to trust God. Each day is a new chance to deepen our trust. I have been helped in my daily trust of God by thinking about each breath that I take. The air we breathe is the same air that Jesus breathed. We are filled with the breath of God every time we breathe. God is in me and all around me. I hope each day to be more aware of this wonder. Take a few moments to focus on your breathing, and give thanks to God for this gift.

Faith grows as we admit our doubts. Is this not what the father in this Gospel story did? He knew he didn't have complete faith, but he offered what he had for the sake of his son. We can be honest with God about our doubts. We can offer them for God's healing, liberating touch. Each day is a day to move from unbelief to belief.

Faith is not simply a content to be learned but a commitment to be lived.
Robert McAfee Brown

We know more faith is demanded of us, so it helps if we can connect ourselves to the community of faith. The Church can help us in our struggle. We hear the stories of how others live out their faith. We ask for prayers. We sing the great hymns of tradition, songs of faith that through the wonder of music and lyrics plant their stories in us. We challenge and console one another as we describe our journeys and reflect on our faithfulness. We laugh and cry together and know that God wants to move us from lamentation to praise.

O for a Thousand Tongues to Sing

O for a thousand tongues to sing my great Redeemer's praise, the glories of my God and King, the triumph of his grace! My gracious Master and my God, assist me to proclaim, to spread thro' all the earth abroad the honors of thy name.
Charles Wesley

Have Faith in God

By the time I met Merry Harter, she was already in her seventies, at least. Her pastor called me and said, "One of my members has moved to your neck of the woods. Why don't you go over to visit her in the nursing home?" I'm ashamed to admit that my first response was, wearily, "Another old person to visit." Was I ever in for an education!

> *If wrinkles must be written upon our brows,*
> *let them not be written upon the heart.*
> *The spirit should never grow old.*
> James A. Garfield

I visited Merry when she had only been at the nursing home for a short time. In her inimitable way, however, she had already organized a weekly Bible study, a monthly worship service, and had signed up to tutor ESL (English as a Second Language) students in reading. Despite the fact that her swollen knees made walking difficult, Merry seemed to be constantly on the go. I may have expected her energy to be withered by age, but I was wrong. Merry was a go-getter with an inner energy that came from her deep faith in God.

> *No matter what stage of life we're at, God can*
> *use us for good in the world. With open hearts,*
> *our lives can bear fruit even if our bodies are no*

*longer youthful or strong. Faith in God keeps
us focused on what really matters: bearing
fruit as followers of Jesus.*

Merry never let herself become depressed because of physical pain or her inability to be active. (When she retired from her nursing career, she volunteered for the Peace Corps in Tanzania!) Out of her deep life of prayer, she focused on what she could still do even when walking was difficult. Faith in God kept Merry's spirit strong, even as her body began to wear down with age and infirmity. What an example to us all!

*   *   *

Dear Lord,

Thank you for giving us the freedom to fail and the grace of forgiveness and restoration. Help us learn from our failures to be more like your Son, Jesus. And knowing that we are perfect only in our Savior, we want to be more compassionate toward our brothers and sisters in Christ who are failing now. We praise you for the loving family you have given us in this church we call our home.

Amen

*   *   *

When Jesus Asks You to Pray

*Then Jesus told them a parable about their
need to pray always and not to lose heart.*
Luke 18:1

The Father's Loving Generosity

Father's Day is a time to remember and celebrate what fathers have contributed to their
children. From a practical standpoint, the focus
during the rest of the year is on the child and his
or her needs and desires. So it seems only right
that fathers and mothers should be lovingly spotlighted from time to time.

Comprehension Takes Time

For the first 18 to 21 (or more!) years of their
lives, children are highly dependent on parents
to provide for their needs. Of course, children
only gradually become aware of just how dependent they are on their parents' provision. (Some,
seemingly, never do.) They are usually caught
up in trying to "grow up" and declare their inde-
pendence.

Because they are thoroughly preoccupied with
their own personal desires or problems, children

...ght to their parents' earnest ...ir needs and to bond with ...the parents painstakingly try ...efforts to them, there usually ...le time before the kids really ...rstand. Rarely will a child start to comprehend before the latter part of high school. Sometimes it begins to dawn on them during the college years. Most of the time, however, it is only when they have children of their own that they really commence to perceive the loving generosity of their own parents.

Bad Examples

Among the greatest tragedies in life are abusive or coldhearted parents who do not meet their children's needs. Certainly, there are many instances in which these people are simply treating their offspring the way they were treated as kids. Unfortunately, that is how they learned about being a parent. As understandable as that may be, it does not diminish the tragic scars and deprivation in the lives of their own precious children.

Sadly, there seem to be many people whose image of God the Father is closer to a coldhearted or even abusive parent than to the loving heavenly Father that he really is. Why is this?

There are, of course, the consistently difficult questions, such as why an all-powerful God would allow bad things to happen to seemingly good people. Beyond that, one of the most common blights on God the Father's good name has to do with prayer.

God's Good Gift

When people make sincere requests before God, why doesn't he always fulfill their requests? As the perfect father, God does not give his children everything they desire or ask for, for what they want is not always the best for them. And yet, he does lovingly meet all the needs of his children. As Jesus said, the heavenly Father would never be like a human parent whose child sought food and instead received a stone or a dangerous snake.

> *Is there anyone among you who, if your child asks for bread, will give a stone? Or if the child asks for a fish, will give a snake? If you then, who are evil, know how to give good gifts to your children, how much more will your Father in heaven give good things to those who ask him!*
> Matthew 7:9–11

The Book of James makes it clear that every good gift ultimately comes from the heavenly Father. God does give good gifts to those who ask him. But that must not be mistaken for some kind of heavenly credit card with no limit. God the Father is not a great big "sugar daddy" in the sky.

With wisdom we realize that just because God wants the best for us does not mean we get everything we request. The good gifts he gives us are the ones that really are good for us. That means many times he answers with something that turns out to be better than what was requested.

> *Sometimes it seems our heartfelt prayers must be falling on deaf ears. Since nothing appears to be happening in response to our requests, does God the Father really want to answer our prayers?*

Wisdom also realizes that timing is everything. Our heavenly Father often does not answer prayers immediately. Instead, God is saving his perfect answer until just the right moment to introduce it into your life.

Next Father's Day, wouldn't it be appropriate to remember your heavenly Father, who loves you enough to always hear you out and who gives you gifts that are perfect for you?

✻   ✻   ✻

Dear Lord,
Thank you that you are a caring father who desires to give good gifts to your children even more than we

want to pray for them. Help us pray according to your will and with patience wait on your perfect timing.

Amen

✳   ✳   ✳

Ask in My Name

On the night he was betrayed, Jesus spent a long evening eating and conversing with the group of friends who knew him best. After what we call the Last Supper, Jesus took the opportunity to share some final teachings with his disciples. We see in these moments a leader who knows he has to say good-bye to his followers, a friend who wants to be sure his friends are equipped to handle a world without his physical presence.

> *Until now you have not asked for anything in my name. Ask and you will receive, so that your joy may be complete.*
> John 16:24

Jesus has often talked to these friends about the power of prayer, but before he was always beside them to pray for them and be the one through whom they understood their connection to God. Jesus knows that it is important for each person to find a personal relationship with the Almighty. "Until now you have not asked for anything in my name. Ask and you will receive, so that your joy may be complete."

For three years, Jesus has been with most of these friends on a day-in, day-out basis. They know him, love him, and trust him. They have heard his stories and know that God is like the woman searching for a lost coin and the shepherd searching for his lost sheep. Only now do they begin to understand that once Jesus is gone, God will still be with them. God's heart of love will always be open to them.

Jesus provides our link for a relationship to God that comes through him but is still personal.

We who live long after Jesus and his friends have left the earth also need a God who personally cares for us and is available through prayer. Our joy is made complete when we connect to God in Jesus' name.

*　　*　　*

Loving God,

Thank you for sending Jesus to earth so we might know you better. Because of him, we understand your love in a new way, and we see that the door to your heart is always open. Help us, when we pray, to always pray in the spirit of Jesus Christ, so we, too, might be ready to listen to you and serve you completely.

Amen

*　　*　　*

No Longer Hypocrites in Prayer

*And whenever you pray, do not be like
the hypocrites; for they love to stand and pray
in the synagogues and at the street corners, so
that they may be seen by others.*
Matthew 6:5

What is your motivation for prayer? This is
the issue that Jesus is addressing. I remember hearing the late Quaker teacher and author
Douglas Steere say that the purpose of prayer is
to bring about change in our whole being. Prayer
is not about being seen or noticed by others but
about a deep relationship with God that manifests
itself in deeds of kindness and words of care.

Jesus assumes you are a person of prayer and
wants you to have the same intimacy with God
that he shares. He has a suggestion: "Do not be
like the hypocrites." Their outer actions do not
correspond with the inner life of prayer. There
are people who use their religion or their church
attendance as a way of winning favor. They want
to be seen as good and upstanding members of
their community. It is good for business. It gives
comfort to the family.

*Jesus is not putting down public prayer,
only showy prayer. Jesus looks at the
motivation of our prayer as well as the
fruits of our relationship with God.*

Jesus looks at the heart. Is there a connection between what is said and what is done? Do the words pronounced so grandly in the public arena match up with deeds of compassion and acts of justice? "What good is it, my brothers and sisters," says James, "if you say you have faith but do not have works?" (James 2:14).

Look at your prayer life. Has your relationship with God led you to be more loving? Are you trying to impress God with your prayers, or are you honestly coming before God in humility and with thanksgiving? Are you finding more peace and joy in your times of prayer?

Unity in Prayer

For me, the most powerful part of our worship service is the prayer time, when we begin by sharing joys (causes for thanksgiving to God) and concerns (specific requests for God's presence and power). The congregation so firmly believes in the power of intercessory prayer that even visitors sometimes raise their hands to share what is heavy on their hearts and have the gathered community offer up prayers.

Praying together brings us together. When we gather in Christian community, God is with us, and suddenly we are not separate individuals but one in Jesus' name.

On any given week, there will be persons lifted up who are ill, who must face the death of a loved one, or who are dealing with depression. No request is unimportant to God and our church. All requests for prayers are lifted up as the community prays together.

In sharing our lives, we get to know each other, and we are bonded by the belief that God hears our prayers and responds. Even when the outcome is not what we want, we trust in God.

> *Again, truly I tell you, if two of you agree on earth about anything you ask, it will be done for you by my Father in heaven. For where two or three are gathered in my name, I am here among them.*
> Matthew 18:19–20

There is sometimes a palpable presence of Jesus among us. Other times, it is more like a warm feeling of being surrounded in love and understanding. But there is never any doubt that the risen Lord stands among us.

I like the image of hot coals: When gathered together, they continue to provide warmth. Separate the coals and they cool. Even the most independent of us benefits from community. God didn't mean for us to go it alone!

Almighty God,

Fulfill now, O Lord, our desires and petitions as may be best for us; granting us in this world knowledge of your truth, and in the age to come life everlasting.

St. John Chrysostom

Deliver Us from Evil Times!

Tornadoes and hurricanes are cousins. The difference is that tornadoes, comparatively, slug away in the lightweight class, while hurricanes usually deliver fearsome knockout punches as powerful heavyweights.

For all their windblown power, tornado funnels swoop down from the sky, cut a narrow swath of destruction, and then lift off again. A person, however, may find safety even a short distance from where a tornado touches down.

By contrast, hurricanes wreak havoc along and behind a front that is hundreds of miles long. Besides the high winds and rain, hurricanes spawn many tornadoes; in fact, any one of those tornadoes can be the most dangerous part of a hurricane.

Fleeing from the path of a hurricane is a much bigger challenge. You may have to hurry hundreds of miles away from it to get completely out of harm's way.

The Boy Scout motto is "Be prepared." If we are praying, and are as prepared as we possibly can be, what is God's role in protecting us during very difficult times?

The Bible realistically tells us that there are periods of suffering that we will all have to endure. That is why Jesus wisely advises us to pray, "Deliver us from evil." Like raging tornadoes that come and go, there are many events that leave an evil path of destruction and pain in our lives.

There will come a time, however, at the end of the age in which we are living, when suffering will be at an all-time high. For that time, or any other period of suffering, Jesus counsels alertness and prayer for escape from the most intense evil and pain.

Be alert at all times, praying that you may have the strength to escape all these things that will take place, and to stand before the Son of Man.
Luke 21:36

Jesus does promise protection, though it's impossible to know exactly how that works. He will tailor the protection to each one's needs and prayers.

*   *   *

Dear Lord,

I know that hard times will come to me. There are always challenges that come our way, and I do not ask that you deliver me from those stretching periods in my life. I only seek your strong protection from the overwhelmingly difficult times so that my faith in you will not falter.

Amen

*   *   *

Jesus, Guide Us

Most mornings I begin a time of prayer with the words of St. Francis. As I sing the words, I am asking for light, faith, hope, charity, insight, and wisdom, so I might see the path of God in the day that is unfolding. It is a prayer for guidance and discernment.

Days can be packed with people to meet and decisions to be made, and throughout the day I desire the guidance of God. I want to make good decisions and treat people kindly. I want to help those in need and avoid temptations. I pray that God will guide me, lead me, and protect me, and that I will serve him faithfully.

We can ask God to lead us and guide us through each day.

When Jesus goes out to the Mount of Olives and instructs his disciples to pray to avoid the time of trial, he is echoing his earlier instructions to pray the following words: "Do not bring us to the time of trial" (Matthew 6:13). This can also be paraphrased as "Save us from the coming trial" or "Do not bring us to the test." They are all ways of asking God to guide us through each day. It is a way of asking God to help us discern what is the right way to go.

> *He came out and went, as was his custom, to the Mount of Olives; and the disciples followed him. When he reached the place, he said to them, "Pray that you may not come into the time of trial."*
> Luke 22:39–40

Another way to sharpen our discernment of the Lord's way is to review each day, looking back over the events and giving thanks or noticing the areas where we fell short. If there is one thing that keeps coming to mind in the review, use that as a focus for prayer. Then look toward the next day and be aware of the events and feelings of anticipation. Offer what is to come to God, and pray that God will guide you and keep you from trials and temptations. Finally, say the Lord's Prayer.

Our Father in heaven,
hallowed be your name.
Your kingdom come.
Your will be done,
on earth as it is in heaven.
Give us this day our daily bread.
And forgive us our debts,
as we also have forgiven our debtors.
And do not bring us to the time of trial,
but rescue us from the evil one.
Matthew 6:9–13

These words that Jesus has given us are filled with spiritual insight. They help us navigate the troubled waters of life. And they keep us faithful to the will of our heavenly Father.

* * *

Most high and glorious God,
Give light to the darkness of my soul.
Give me right faith, certain hope, and perfect charity.
Lord, give me insight and wisdom,
So I might always discern
Your holy and true will.
Amen

* * *

When Jesus Asks You to Love

*I give you a new commandment, that you love
one another. Just as I have loved you, you
also should love one another.*
John 13:34

Put Your Heart into It

Have you ever seen this bumper sticker? "God
said it. I believe it. That settles it." I'm always
a little put off by this message. Is it suggesting that
God doesn't expect us to use our minds? Should
we avoid questions in favor of blind faith?

Love God with All Your Mind

*And one of them, a lawyer, asked him a question
to test him. "Teacher, which commandment in
the law is the greatest?" He said to him, "'You shall
love the Lord your God with all your heart, and
with all your soul, and with all your mind.' This is
the greatest and first commandment."*
Matthew 22:35–38

Here Jesus indicates that we are to use everything
we are—our hearts, souls, and minds—to love
God. Perhaps a better phrase would be: "God
loves me. I believe it. That settles it."

While there is much debate over the interpretation of these three parts of a person, let's assume that our hearts represent the emotional, inner feeling aspect of ourselves; that our souls represent the spiritual, God-conscious component; and that minds represent our intellectual capacity.

Jesus came not to destroy the old commandments but to fulfill and amplify them. He boiled down all the regulations of the Law of Moses into a new commandment found in these verses: We are to love God with everything we are and have.

When I read these verses, I find it much easier to love God in the reverse order of Jesus' statement. In a Western culture that primarily identifies itself with linguistic and logical modes of thinking, it is not surprising that loving God with my mind seems to be the easiest of the three. Obviously we can use our minds to study God's Word, the writings of Church historians, and inspirational material (like this book!). We can all think thoughts of love and appreciation for God without much effort.

As I meditated on these verses, for example, and focused on how much I love God, I thought about all he has done for me, the ways he has guided my life, and his words of love in the Scriptures. I concluded that I love God because he first loved me, and that his is a great big love that has provided a way for imperfect me to live eternally with the Perfect One.

Love God with All Your Soul

To love God with my soul or spiritual side has not seemed so difficult either. Maybe that's because I have a God who is pursuing a loving relationship with me. Growing up in a home where my parents loved God helped create in me the spiritual values of church attendance, Bible study, personal prayer, development and use of my spiritual gifts, and more. Early in my childhood, I felt God's stirring in my soul, drawing me toward him through his love. After 40 years of spiritual development, I've learned I can best love God with all my soul by obeying his Word and worshiping him with other believers.

Love God with All Your Heart

This brings me to Jesus' first charge—to love God with all my heart. Certainly Jesus expects me to be rational and vigorous in my love for God. Unfortunately, I often unconsciously interpret his command to mean that I am to love God as a mere act of the will without any emotional attachment. After all, the Greek verb for love in these verses is not *phileo*, which means friendly affection, but *agapao*, the commitment of devotion.

Yet, in normal ancient Greek usage, *agape* had a number of meanings, including "to long for" or "to prefer." Do I long for God as a child longs for a parent? I have to admit that sometimes I don't. And I'm probably not the only person who often wonders, "Why don't I feel love toward God?"

What many of us are experiencing is a fragmented love. Somehow, we have to find a way to integrate the longing of our spirits and minds with our innermost, heartfelt feelings.

Falling in Love with God

My husband, Stan, and I were very good friends for a long time before we fell in love. We attended the same university, played tennis together, and spent a lot of time together in a college Bible study group. After a year of intimate friendship, the idea of what it might be like to be in love with Stan began creeping into my thoughts on a regular basis. Those invasive thoughts led to a longing to be with Stan. Once that desire was reciprocated, we began to experience more heart-intensive feelings for each other. In fact, we couldn't get enough time together, and our relationship was (and continues to be) characterized by challenging each other's mind, spirit, and passion.

In the same way, spending time with God enriches and deepens our relationship with him. The more we get to know him and experience his love, the more we will be able to love him with our entire being. Then we will long for time alone with him because we love him and enjoy his fellowship.

> *O Love, were I but love, And could I but love you, Love, with love! O Love, for love's sake, grant that I, Having become love, may know Love wholly as Love!*
> Hadewijch of Belgium

Maybe one of the reasons Jesus commanded us to first love God with all our hearts is because he knows that a deep, inner relationship must set the tone for loving God with our souls and minds. It is not enough to think about loving God. It is not enough to believe that we should love God. It is not enough to work at proving our love for God. But if we open ourselves up to a love relationship with God, I believe our hearts will be transformed and we will begin to experience the passion for him that Jesus commanded.

Loving Obedience

Our love for Jesus manifests itself in our thoughts, words, and actions. When we truly love him, it becomes clear how we should act. Even when we feel tempted to do the less-than-loving thing, we can remember Jesus' love for us and follow his example.

Flora's Godly Glow

Four-year-old Flora is the kind of kid who makes people glad just to be alive when they see her shining face. Strangers must look at her and think, "Today's a good day, after all." Flora is good at hugs and verbal affirmations. She takes time with people, looks deep into their eyes, and listens carefully to their responses.

Flora frequently bounces into my office, full of energy and questions about God. One day she said, "I asked my dad what a minister does and he said you teach about God." I nodded. "That's a big part of my job."

Flora looked serious. "I want to teach about God when I grow up." I hugged her to me. "Oh, Flora, you already do teach about God." "I do?" she asked. "You are so full of love and goodness, how can people not know God if they know you?" I answered.

She chortled with delight, then bounced out of my office back to the nursery school playground. I sat, realizing the truth of what I had said to her: What a difference we can make to the world when our love shines out from us! I can't help but think that Jesus was the sort of person whose presence made ordinary people feel special, unreligious types want to know God, the unrighteous yearn for justice. His very life was an example of what it means to follow all the commandments.

Live Like Jesus

If you love me, you will keep my commandments.
John 14:15

And so, when he tells us, "If you love me, you will keep my commandments," we know that only by such obedience do we really show our love. Sure, there are difficult people whom we find hard to love. That's when we let Jesus love through us until our own love develops. There will be situations where it would be easiest to fudge a bit on our Christian morals ("I won't point out that the salesclerk gave me too much change"; "I'll pretend I didn't hear that racist joke"; "If I cheat on my wife just this once ... "). But our love for Jesus helps us keep his commandments.

Is there someone you find difficult to love? Imagine Jesus in that person. Make an effort to discover something lovable about them that might not be easily visible. Pray for the person so that you might feel connected to them through the spirit of Jesus, who came that they—as well as you—might know God.

If there is any kindness I can show, or any good thing I can do to any fellow being, let

*me do it now, and not deter or neglect it, as
I shall not pass this way again.*
William Penn

Are there other commandments that you find hard to honor? Find strength in Jesus, who loved you so much he was willing to die for you. If God was able to raise Jesus from the dead, then certainly God can provide you with the wherewithal to stand strong in your beliefs.

Believe in Jesus. Live like Jesus. Love like Jesus.

*When you love you should not say, "God is in my
heart," but rather, "I am in the heart of God."*
Kahlil Gibran

Love God, Love Others

I learned about loving service from my parents. Their Christian faith was not a "Sundays only" practice. They lived it all through the week, and as a young child I sometimes found that difficult. Often my mom would bake three apple pies. The smell would fill the whole house, and I would dream of eating my favorite pie for days, only to discover that my mom was taking one to a neighbor and another to a church potluck. I would be left to share one with my family.

Many of the Christmas cookies disappeared the same way. There were always some for me, though maybe not as many as my greedy eyes desired. I look back now and give thanks that my parents modeled sharing. I sometimes joke with my mom that she took the words of Jesus literally when he said, "Feed my lambs."

> *When they had finished breakfast, Jesus said to Simon Peter, "Simon son of John, do you love me more than these?" He said to him, "Yes, Lord; you know that I love you." Jesus said to him, "Feed my lambs."*
> John 21:15

Jesus and Scripture are clear that love of God should lead to loving action. If we love God, then we will love others. Indeed, when Jesus was summing up the commandments, he clearly linked these two: "You shall love the Lord your God with all your heart, and with all your soul, and with all your mind" and "You shall love your neighbor as yourself" (Matthew 22:37, 39).

Loving service will sometimes take us to people and places we don't expect. Peter did not expect to take Christianity to Gentiles, but being nudged in a dream and receiving the visitors sent by Cornelius (Acts 10) led him to a dramatic change. "I truly understand that God shows no partiality, but in every nation anyone who fears him and does what is right is acceptable to him" (Acts 10:34–35). God's love crosses all boundaries, and such a vision has sent doctors, teachers, plumbers, and builders all over the world to extend love and care to people in need.

If we love God, we are led to love others.
The two go hand in hand and lead us
to some surprising ministries.

Loving service takes us to forgotten people. Friends of mine have started a summer week of camp for people with AIDS. Ministers, nurses, and volunteers create a week of fun, relaxation, and worship for people who may not be around to enjoy the next summer. A church youth group visits a nursing home and discovers that one of their kids, who is often in trouble, has a real knack for befriending the residents in their wheelchairs.

It all starts with the love of God and learning to discern whom God would have you love. "Do you love me? Feed the hungry, care for the sick, embrace the forgotten, care for the homeless, love the unlovable."

*　　*　　*

Compassionate God,

Give us eyes to see those who are in need, and make our hearts tender to the pain around us.

Give us a patient persistence to see that justice is done and fill us with a gentle courage to care when it would be easier to turn away.

Teach us, loving God, to follow the compassionate steps of your Son, who loved us so deeply that we can truly love others.

Amen

*   *   *

Loving Your Enemies Is Healthy

In Jesus' day, people heard established teachers in their society say they were to love their neighbors—that is, their families, their friends, and others living nearby. In teaching this principle, the rabbis were doing no more than applying the straightforward wording of the Hebrew Bible.

Hate Those Who Hate You?

So far, so good. But some teachers did not stop there. It was undoubtedly their observation of human nature that convinced them that hating enemies was acceptable. But the Bible has never given the okay to such hatred.

> *It is at least as common to hear a small child scream "I hate you!" as to hear "I love you!" Why should you even try to change something that is so deep-seated in the human personality?*

This appears to be a case where the conventional logic won out over time. Perhaps there was initial hesitancy to make the jump from loving those on your side to hating those on the opposing side, but eventually the natural tendency of human nature won out. It came to the point where hating those who hate you made as much sense to the bulk of society as loving those who love you.

From a nearsighted perspective, that may pass for wisdom. Jesus, however, knew better. Hatred is unwise both because it is wrong and because it is unhealthy. The Bible offers a large number of cases in which people hate one another. Though there are many occasions in which no comment is made as to the rightness or wrongness of the hatred, that does not mean the Scriptures are quiet.

There are no situations in which interpersonal hatred is considered right (even if it is under-standable). There are, however, enough instances in which the hate is clearly labeled as wrong to get the point. Whenever the Bible chooses to speak to the issue, it leaves no doubt that one person hating another is wrong.

Proper Hatred

Yet, there is one broad category in which hatred is always right. But it still does not allow for hating other people. Rather, proper hatred is hating sin. That means hating the act, but not the actor; it means hating that which is done in violation of God's gracious standards, not hating the person who commits the sinful action.

That, of course, is not an easy thing to do. It almost seems like splitting hairs to try to tell the difference between what has been done and who has done it. After all, the wrongful action would not have happened if the person involved had not chosen to act.

It appears that God has wisely laid out this distinction between sin and sinner for two important reasons. First, the Lord hates the sin, but does not hate the sinner. Thus, for human beings to do likewise is to choose to be in God's camp and to reflect in our lives a truly divine perspective.

Second, and extremely significant psychologically, hating the act but not the person provides a way to channel the outrage that is felt. That, of course, is no small thing. It is possible to defuse hate, but it is much more common to internalize it. It is much better to properly express outrage as hatred of an action than to bury it inside as a virtual volcano of bitterness toward the person performing the act.

A Tall Order

> *You have heard that it was said, "You shall love your neighbor and hate your enemy." But I say to you, Love your enemies and pray for those who persecute you.*
> Matthew 5:43–44

Jesus corrected the improper assertion that it is good to hate one's enemies with his own authoritative command. Loving your enemies, including those who persecute you, is a tall order. It is much easier to give in to hate. However, loving is clearly the right thing to do; both psychologically and physically, it is the healthy thing to do.

It is no longer a mystery why bitter people are more likely to experience heart disease, ulcers, strokes, and other physical complications. There is a tremendous amount of internal stress related to hatred. And it is not too much to say that hatred-induced stress eats a person up from the inside out.

Physical problems, premature aging, and—as a worst-case scenario—death before your time are incredibly steep prices to pay for hatred. That remains true no matter what some enemy has done to you.

It should be realized, however, that Jesus is not just asking for a releasing or refocusing of the hatred that is felt toward enemies. He is also insisting on loving prayer for the person that you would much rather despise. If choosing not to hate is a tall order, this assignment is at least as high as the top of a skyscraper!

Forgiveness Is the Key

There is an angle, or at least a perspective, that can make this kind of prayer somewhat easier. Releasing hatred of your enemy, or even someone you care about, requires forgiveness. That is very difficult, but it should be remembered that the person seething with hatred requires forgiveness too.

Think about it. Hatred is sinful, and in committing that sin, you have become an enemy of God's standards. If you must ask God's forgiveness for the sin of bitter hatred, how can you, in good conscience, withhold forgiveness from your enemy?

Hating your enemy requires you to pray to the Lord, asking his forgiveness. So, while you're at it, you might as well go ahead and pray for the enemy who has stirred up your hate. The words may choke up in your heart, if not your throat, as you attempt to express your prayer. The prayer may not be heartfelt initially, but go ahead and do it anyway.

Always remember that it is the right thing, the loving thing, the wise thing to do, almost miraculously so. Also, understand that the Lord will respond to your prayers by eventually enabling you to truly love that previously unlovable enemy.

*   *   *

Dear Lord,

I don't like the idea of not being able to hate my enemy. There is something in me that wants to hate them for what they have done to me or for who they are. Because of this feeling and because of my own sins, I am in great need of your forgiveness. Please help me love my enemy as you want me to do.

Amen

*   *   *

A Friend in Need

We have heard it said: "A friend in need is a friend indeed." Friends with whom you have only been through good times are untested friends. It would be premature, however, to label such people "fair-weather friends" simply because you haven't faced the foul weather of life alongside them yet. Likewise, should you write off someone as a fair-weather friend if they aren't there at the beginning of your troubles? There are many reasons why a friend might not come immediately.

At the Tomb of Lazarus

What are we to make of Jesus' delay in coming to help Lazarus? He was a distance away when he heard about his friend's illness. Still, he did not immediately go upon receiving the news.

> *Jesus began to weep. So the Jews said,*
> *"See how he loved him!"*
> John 11:35–36

In fact, Jesus arrived after Lazarus's funeral. His friend's body had already been in the tomb for several days. While Jesus' tears before the tomb indicated the depth of his loving friendship with Lazarus, some onlookers understandably questioned Jesus' tardy arrival.

It is difficult to understand why Jesus did not appear in time to help Lazarus before he died. And yet, Lazarus's dead body did offer the opportunity for Jesus to perform an amazing miracle of resurrection, one which previewed his own rise from the dead. Beyond the grief of their loss, Lazarus's sisters and friends experienced the joy of getting their beloved brother back.

A Friend Like Jesus

And so it is with our lives. After a tragedy has devastated our lives, the first wave of friends often disappears just as the numbness and shock begin to give way to so many confusing and painful emotions. It is the friend, like Jesus, who is there for you in this even more difficult "foul-weather" phase that qualifies with flying colors as a friend indeed.

How can the love of a friend endure
the worst of times as well as flourish
in the best of times?

There may be reasons why a loving friend might not appear early, and many of those reasons we cannot understand. But when the dust settles from life's stormiest hours, the loving friend will be there when needed most. And so, it is important for us to do what Jesus asks us to do in these difficult situations—and that is to love as he loves. It is in those moments that we will be transformed.

*   *   *

Dear God,

Help me be the kind of friend who weeps when my friends weep and who rejoices when they rejoice. Help me be like Jesus, who is the best friend a person can have. Thank you for your love and for the power to love.

Amen

*   *   *

When Jesus Asks You Not to Worry

*So do not worry about tomorrow, for
tomorrow will bring worries of its own.
Today's trouble is enough for today.*
Matthew 6:34

God Will Provide

J esus understands our mundane worries about
food, shelter, and clothing. While the people
he walked with didn't have to think about health
insurance premiums, income taxes, and pension
plans, those who lived at that "simpler" time
needed reminding that life is more than food, and
the body is more than clothing.

The Blessing of Simplicity

A year's sabbatical spent in a Quaker community
provided an important reminder for our family.
My husband and I, along with our daughter, took
a year to be students of the spiritual life instead
of pastors. We went from two full-time incomes
to no income. We left a three-bedroom home in
California for two rooms in a large house at a
Pennsylvania Quaker center. We put most of our
earthly belongings in a 100-square-foot self-storage

space, packing our Honda Civic with only what we needed to live for a year with our three-year-old daughter and our soon-to-be-born son.

Do not worry about your life, what you will eat or what you will drink, or about your body, what you will wear. Is not life more than food, and the body more than clothing?
Matthew 6:25

Talk about simplifying! For music, we packed our ten favorite tapes, and we chose a small sampling of books to get us through the year. Most of the items we had thought necessary for our daughter's infancy had long since been sold, but when our son was born we managed just fine without them.

One of our "new" rooms was furnished with three beds and a dresser. The other was a "great room": kitchen (hot plate and slow cooker), dining room (table and chairs), living room (couch), study (desk), and guest room (mattress on the floor).

Happiness resides not in possessions and not in gold; the feeling of happiness dwells in the soul.
Democritus

Do we remember that as a year of hardship? Absolutely not! We remember the way the sun streamed through large windows in both rooms, the generosity of the Quaker community, the joy of a newborn child, and the wonder of a preschooler. During the year, we had very few moments of wanting more things. In some ways, it was a burden to come back to the storage space and a three-bedroom home.

Let God Provide

That sabbatical year was a perfect chance for us to immerse ourselves in the goodness of God's generosity. The goal of that year was to focus on God's presence in our lives. We were the lilies in the field, the sparrows in the air, the creatures God cared for. We learned to trust that God would provide for us. Rather than spending time worrying about money, we did our part (finding part-time work, letting churches know we were available to speak) and then "let go and let God" provide.

Jesus promises that God will provide for all our needs. When we spend time worrying, we doubt God's power to work in our lives. It's up to us to give our best effort and then trust in God to care for us.

If you feel anxious, take time to sit in a restful place and watch the birds. Do they look worried? Learn from their joyous living. Admire the flowers. Isn't the span of their days beautiful? So why not trust that our generous God will know our needs and care for us all our days?

Worried to Death

As the TV blared in the background, I picked up the phone. I think my heart was pounding louder than the bellowing of the television. As I expected, my doctor was at the other end of the line. "Your biopsy report came back, and I have some bad news." I'm sure anyone who has heard those words can empathize with my response—shock, fear, tears, grief, worry—though not necessarily in that order.

A Lifetime of Worry

I have spent most of my life worrying. I worried about my health, my family, what other people think, what to wear tomorrow, what I will have for dinner, the future, old age, and even about my little dog, Thera. When I turned 35, my deepest thought was "My life is half over, and I still have so much I want to do!"

A year later, I was diagnosed with cancer, and I angrily (and mistakenly) imagined God saying, "I'll really give you something to worry about!" Most of my previous worries and fears had been unfounded. Now I faced the real possibility of a terminal illness, which caused me to take a long, hard look inward.

For the next several weeks, as I prepared for surgery, I began to realize that the length of my life was well beyond my control, and surprisingly, peace settled over me like a cozy warm quilt. It was a disarming calmness; I had to trust God and allow him to hold my life in his hands. Worrying was futile. It could not change my illness or my situation. I could not add one hour to my life by worrying.

> *And can any of you by worrying add*
> *a single hour to your span of life?*
> Matthew 6:27

My previous worryings hadn't prevented a diagnosis of cancer. In fact, medical professionals tell us we may even be subtracting time from our lives through worry and stress. Anxiety is thought to cause elevated blood pressure, increased risk of heart disease, digestive problems, and more. I decided that after the surgery I would make a good recovery and put worrying about the life-threatening disease out of my mind.

Welcomed News

As I lay in the hospital bed, drowsy from a morphine drip, the phone rang. Again it was my doctor's voice. "I have the reports back from your surgery. The cancer was contained, and no additional treatment is necessary."

Relief did not really settle in until weeks later, as I began to realize I was going to live—at least for a little while longer. The weeks of recovery following surgery gave me plenty of time to reflect on how to live in the present rather than worry about dying in the future.

> *In a world plagued with fear of growing old, Jesus' words regarding worry are timeless. He encourages us to seek the spiritual benefits of belonging to God, including contentment in the knowledge that he knows the length of our days.*

I think living without worry comes with a great deal of practice. Perhaps we should examine what it is that prevents us from trusting the Lord to help us cope with our anxious thoughts about life and death. Then, when we find ourselves worrying, let it serve as a reminder that we are trusting ourselves and our own abilities rather than trusting God.

Are you worried and in distress today? Whether you're troubled about something big or small, worrying won't change your situation. Jesus does not say that bad things will not happen to us, but he does invite us to rest in his arms. As we trust God to carry the burdens of our health, families, finances, and so on, we can discover the comfort, security, and peace of knowing that God takes care of his own.

God Holds the Future

God holds the future, He's got a plan, there's
no need to worry, 'cause it's all in His hand.
So if you are strugglin' with what you
should do, God holds the future for you.
David Meece and Brown Bannister

Faith to Face Natural Fears

What is fear? The dictionary describes it as a distressing emotion or anxiety in the face of impending (or at least possible) pain or danger. This definition, however, seems a little narrow. Fear can take on many forms.

Afraid but Not Fearful

But the angel said to the women, "Do not be afraid; I
know that you are looking for Jesus who was crucified.
He is not here; for he has been raised, as he said."
Matthew 28:5–6

As the women headed to the tomb of Jesus early that Sunday morning, the apostles were fearfully huddled behind closed doors. They were in hiding because they were afraid of being arrested by the Jewish authorities who had sentenced Jesus to death just days before.

Clearly, fearfulness did not paralyze these women. They possessed the courage and faith to go and pay their respects at the earliest possible moment. Going to the tomb on the Jewish Sabbath or overnight would have been improper for them. Therefore, they had to wait until Sunday at dawn. Nevertheless, nothing was going to stop them from going as soon as it was permissible.

These women lived in a society with a strong belief that angels were very active in the affairs of humankind. In fact, most of Jewish society in that day (except the religious group called the Sadducees) firmly believed in the resurrection of the dead.

Also, in thinking of the resurrection, there had been the teaching of Jesus. Not only did he teach the truthfulness of the resurrection in general, but he had also raised several people from the dead during his ministry. There had been the son of the widow in Nain, then Jairus's daughter, and finally Jesus' close friend Lazarus. Further, Jesus had stated repeatedly that he himself would be killed and raised from the dead.

Therefore, it was probably not the idea of angels, the raising of the dead, or even the resurrection of Jesus that caused the women to be afraid. Rather, the reality of the angel and the empty tomb caught them off guard. When they encountered the actuality of what they believed, it took their breath away.

Fear Is Natural

Some people would say that you don't really
have faith or confidence if you feel fear at any
point. That sort of fearlessness is, unfortunately,
an unrealistic expectation for most people. For
example, even the most polished and confident
athletes and speakers frequently admit to still
feeling butterflies in their stomachs just hours
prior to a game or speech. Sometimes they will
even go so far as to say that they would think
something was wrong with them if they weren't
feeling that fear to some extent. So, if such
accomplished masters are typically nervous and
fearful, why should the rest of us be embarrassed
or sheepish when we feel the same thing?

Let's face it. The real argument is not about
whether someone should be fearful. Fear, to some
extent, is a completely natural response. Rather,
the question should be about what people should
do when they feel fear, when their pulse and
breathing quicken, when the hair stands up on the
back of their neck.

Fear Leads to Faith and to God

The wisdom that comes from Jesus is to use
natural fear as a springboard to faith. Not only
does the Bible recognize the common reality
of fear in our lives, but the Hebrew Scriptures

frequently even refer to what is often called "the fear of the Lord." This terminology partly has to do with respecting the greatness and holiness of God. A healthy fear of the rightful judge of the universe is a positive thing.

Some people feel fear at the drop of a hat. Yet, as extreme as that sounds, it is even more unnatural not to feel fear at all. From the standpoint of wisdom, what is the proper role of fear?

It is highly unlikely, however, that having respect, no matter how great that respect is, can ever be an expression of the full meaning of "the fear of the Lord." Instead, this key concept almost surely includes focusing the natural fear you are feeling toward the Lord. You can do so and not only realize that he deserves your respectful fear but also trust that he will calm your fears regarding any dangers in your life.

It is unlikely that many of us will ever stand face-to-face with an angel or walk into a graveyard and be informed that a resurrection has taken place. Yet, there will inevitably be surprises, shocks, or dangers that will stir up fear in each of our lives. In wisdom, we must put aside the question of why we are fearful. We must channel our fear in the direction of the Lord, who will put our emotions in the calm eye of the storm.

* * *

Lord,

Whether I admit it or not, I am fearful. Please help me to face my fears head-on and then to act in faith.

Amen

* * *

Faith Overcomes Fear

During a Bible study, one of my parishioners commented on the disciples. "They actually lived with Jesus, knew him personally, heard him speak. Yet still, they constantly misunderstood him. Their faith was so small. You'd think you'd stay on your toes if you were hanging out with Jesus!"

Freedom from Fear

Perhaps the disciples are a gift to us because we can identify with them when they did not understand the meaning of Jesus' words. We'd prefer to ignore certain passages of Scripture because the words are just too difficult to put into action. Like the disciples, we have moments when we lack faith. If we had been "hanging out with Jesus," we, too, probably would have been terrified to see the risen Christ come into the locked room where we were hiding out.

The previous days had been fraught with grief over the death of their beloved leader and fear that the Roman authorities might discover their relationship to Jesus. Would the Romans take them away to be interrogated and then hang them on a cross? The men and women who had followed Jesus hardly knew which way to turn. They were talking about the supposed appearance of Jesus to two of their number. Had he really joined them on the road to Emmaus? Had they truly recognized him in the breaking of the bread?

Jesus understands our fears and wants us to know that no matter what happens in our lives, he is with us. When we believe in his power, fear has no hold on us.

All these questions were churning in their minds, and suddenly there he was. "Peace be with you" (Luke 24:36), he said, but they felt far from peaceful. "They were startled and terrified, and thought that they were seeing a ghost" (verse 37). We understand such fear, for we have often been fearful ourselves. It wasn't until Jesus named their fear, their doubts, their lack of understanding that his voice began to sound familiar. When he instructed them to look at his wounded hands and feet, they recognized the wounds of love and knew that their beloved Jesus was with them again.

Why did Jesus come back? He knew these people and their needs. He understood their obvious fear, and he wanted to give them the gift of a peace that would last forever. His earthly presence had helped them feel secure; now he wanted them to feel his spirit even when his body was no longer present. Jesus had talked about peace before, but it was only in this context of true terror (would they be discovered?) that the disciples had a frame of reference that allowed them to put their whole faith in Jesus. Sometimes we most keenly experience God's peace when we are in a time of trial.

A Mother's Faith

I learned a great deal about strength of faith when my mother was diagnosed with inoperable cancer. Her longtime doctor's tears streamed down his face when he told her, "There comes a time in every human's life when medical science can do no more for them. Wanda, I'm sorry to tell you that time is here for you." After he and the rest of my family left the room, I asked my mother how she was feeling.

> *I do not fear to tread the path I cannot see
> Because the hand of One who loves is leading me.*
> Nyata

"I'm so glad I was raised in a Christian home," she responded. "God has been with me through all my life, and my faith in God is strong. God will see me through whatever is to come." Throughout the weeks until her death, my mother's faith never wavered. God had sustained her through the deaths of her father, brother, and son. God would be with her until her earthly end. Her faith reminded everyone around her that "Even though I walk through the darkest valley, I fear no evil; for you are with me" (Psalm 23:4).

Safely Anchored

Think back to a time in your life when you felt fearful. Were you afraid of physical violence? Did you face a serious operation and wonder how it would turn out? Were there personal or financial problems that pressed in on you until you thought you couldn't breathe? What was your experience of God during this difficult time?

When I was in high school, a youth minister used an image that has stuck with me. He said that living in faith was like being on a huge ship with all of the world's people as inhabitants. The vessel was tossed and turned on gigantic waves that terrified many passengers. "Surely we will die!" they screamed. With every wave that crashed into the sides of the boat, some people cringed in terror. Others calmly waited for the storm to blow itself out. They were unaffected by the churning of the sea.

Why was it that some aboard the ship could be calm when others thought they would soon be dead? The ones at peace were those who believed in God's protection. They realized that, though the boat tossed and turned in the storm, it was firmly anchored on a sandbar. No storm could capsize the ship; the sandbar of God's love kept it safely anchored.

I remember thinking how sad it must have been for those who screamed in terror. But what peace there is for us who receive God's love!

*   *   *

Dear Lord,

It sometimes seems as though I'm swimming against the current, and I'm afraid of becoming exhausted and drowning. Please be with me and help me get through the storm.

Amen

*   *   *

Confident of Spiritual Protection

When you hear the word *persecution*, you tend to think of harassment, often violence.

The reason is that violent religious persecution, such as the horrors of the Holocaust, is highly profiled. The number of deaths and the tragedy of starving prisoners catches the attention of many sensitive, caring people.

In the world you face persecution. But take courage; I have conquered the world!
John 16:33

This may be the primary sense in which Jesus is referring to persecution. After all, Jesus and his disciples suffered ever more harassment until finally Jesus was crucified. And after Jesus rose from the dead and ascended into heaven, authorities intimidated the apostles, physically tortured them, and, in most cases, executed them for their faith in the Lord. Similar instances of persecution have taken place throughout the history of the Church.

Persecution, however, is not always brought about by a particular group of people. It is actually far more common for persecution to take place one-on-one. Moreover, persecution may sometimes take subtle forms, such as teasing or making fun of someone's beliefs. In such intimidating situations, it is difficult to stand up for one's faith. This is often because you feel as though you are all alone.

The world in which we live is an increasingly dangerous place, with fewer and fewer exceptions as time passes. Can you ever really feel safe?

If you believe in Jesus, who was brutally persecuted but was raised from the dead, you are never alone. He has conquered death and everything the world can throw at you. Take courage! You are on the winning team, forever and ever.

*   *   *

Dear Lord,

Even the thought of persecution creates fear in my heart. But I thank you that you strengthen my faith in these frightening times. I also thank you for your assurance that all will turn out for the best for me because you are in complete control of both the world and my life. Help me share this faith with others, for as I share, my faith is strengthened as well.

Amen

*   *   *

When Jesus Asks You Not to Judge

For with the judgment you make you will be judged, and the measure you give will be the measure you get.
Matthew 7:2

Consequences and Judgment

Woe to you, Chorazin! Woe to you, Bethsaida! For if the deeds of power done in you had been done in Tyre and Sidon, they would have repented long ago in sackcloth and ashes. But I tell you, on the day of judgment it will be more tolerable for Tyre and Sidon than for you.
Matthew 11:21–22

The Greek word translated "woe" contains the notion of sorrowful pity and anger; thus the interpretation that Jesus shows anger resulting from a saddened heart. Chorazin's and Bethsaida's citizenry did not repent. Jesus says that two cities known for corruption—Tyre and Sidon—would certainly have changed their ways if they had witnessed the miracles he was performing.

When Jesus began his public ministry, he called his listeners to change. "The time is fulfilled, and the kingdom of God has come near; repent, and believe in the good news" (Mark 1:15). He carried this message to cities and towns, from Galilee in the north to Jerusalem in the south. We do not know very much about Chorazin or Bethsaida, but Jesus stopped at both towns. The inhabitants heard his message, saw "deeds of power," and went on their way. They did not respond or change their ways. We do not know the evidence of their refusals, but we know that Jesus was troubled.

We Are Like Chorazin and Bethsaida

Have we also failed to respond to God's call? I think about the busyness of life, full calendars, active families, and even active church life. We are often so busy and tired that when we stop to listen to God, we can be too weary to hear him. Other times, when we do hear God, we choose not to respond or act. When we neglect what God leads us to do, are we really any different from the people of Chorazin or Bethsaida?

There are consequences to our decisions, just as we teach our children that there are consequences to their actions. If you touch the hot stove, you will get hurt. If you eat too much candy, you will not feel well. If you hit another child, there will be a time-out. Children learn cause and effect as it relates to behavior.

When we refuse to become children of God, we experience consequences. First of all, the

*heart of Jesus breaks when we do not respond
to his invitation. Then there are the
rewards that we miss out on.*

Jesus is saying there are consequences in refusing to repent, consequences that affect our daily life. We will miss out on the love, joy, and peace bestowed on his followers. We will not be a part of the community of faith that holds its members accountable and offers guidance and assistance. We will not know the intimacy of prayer. We will feel the loneliness of the world. And we miss out on all of these blessings because we are . . . too busy? Not interested? Too many other things to do first?

Jesus Beckons Us

Jesus is passionately concerned about us. He wants us to know and follow God's way. He wants us to repent and change our ways. To experience the wholeness of life, life as God intended it, we must give ourselves over to him. Otherwise we miss out on God's precious gifts.

Remember that Jesus came into the world not to condemn us but to save us (John 3:16–17). He offered his life for us. God's judgment is tempered with mercy. Now is the perfect time to accept the Good News of Christ!

*   *   *

Loving God,

Open my eyes to your wonders: the magic of birds flying, the power of a sunrise, the glory of a blooming rose. I have witnessed your awesome deeds, and I want you to take my life and make it whole.

Amen

*   *   *

Rocky Relationships

In any print media, such as advertising, magazine production, book publishing, and newspapers, there are often struggles between art directors and editors. The art staff often wants more space for art, and the editor often wants more space on the page for text. There is sometimes conflict on projects, and in the end, it seems as though our biases and opinions remain unchanged. Many art directors with whom I've worked are concrete thinkers, but most remain in the esoteric world of the creative thinker.

Editorial directors, like myself, are often vision-aries who develop concepts we hope will be successful—not just in sales but also in buyer impact. We stake our reputations on firm hunches and customer research. While we want to meet customer needs, we often have our own agenda.

I don't mean to imply that no art directors are visionary abstract thinkers, nor do I mean to say that editorial directors are never in touch with visual elements. Each side is driven by various energies—but it's only natural that tensions and disputes develop.

My Options at Work

When my boss resigned and an art director was promoted to vice president—and my boss— my heart sank. We already had a rocky relationship; he even tried to bar me from product development meetings. He seemed to view me as obstinate, and no doubt I was at times. On the other hand, he allowed his irritation with me to cloud the fact that I was a valuable asset to the company with much to contribute. It probably didn't help that he had publicly stated that he didn't want to work closely with a woman. How would he deal with me now that I reported directly to him? Aaagh!

I thought about my options:

Option #1—I could resign from my position and be free from the stress of working out a difficult relationship. Of course, my job would just be the first in a series of losses. Without my income, I would lose my car, my house, my computer (my only means of freelance income), and my self-esteem. I would be trading the freedom from daily stress at work for the anxiety of worrying about paying the bills at the end of the month.

Option #2—I could ask for a new supervisor, but that would probably mean a reassignment, a demotion, and a cut in pay. I didn't want to watch the projects I was excited about fall through the cracks when I moved on. And a demotion would have felt like a surrender to my new boss's power tactics.

Option #3—I could stick it out and distance myself as much as possible from my new boss. But I still needed his approval for some of my projects, my strategic five-year plan, my budget, and even my vacations. It would be impossible to dodge him forever.

Option #4—I could negotiate for a new relationship with him that was based on mutual respect and a wipe-the-slate-clean approach. I could compromise by forgetting that we had been antagonistic peers and assure him that I would be a supportive employee in spite of our combative history.

Taking Option #4

A week after the announcement of his promotion, I found myself summoned to my new boss's office.

After he said a few general things about the new directions in which he planned to take the company, he asked me if I had anything in response.

The tension in my back was causing my head to throb as I raised my white flag and laid out Option #4. I finished by telling the man that while we had experienced some strained moments together and had our differences in opinion, I hoped he and I would be willing to let go of the past and move toward a more agreeable future.

For Jesus peace seems to have meant not the absence of struggle but the presence of love.
Frederick Buechner

I sat there relieved that I had done my best to make peace. Meanwhile, my new boss leaned back in his chair and said nothing for several long moments. Finally, he grinned, and in an arrogant tone he said, "Well, I don't think you are really capable of change, so we'll just have to see how things go."

That was not the response I had expected or hoped for.

Yet I walked out of his office knowing that I had chosen the right option. I had made the effort to settle my past accounts with this man. Sadly, he didn't seem to want reconciliation.

At first, I was angry and deeply hurt by his critical comments. I wanted what was best for the company, but he rebuffed me, and his stinging words upset me. Later, however, a sense of peace came over me as I realized that I *am* capable of change. I could let go of my past with him. I would treat him with respect and be supportive . . . even if he was unable or unwilling to respond in the same way to me.

The Jesus Option

> *And why do you not judge for yourselves what is right? Thus, when you go with your accuser before a magistrate, on the way make an effort to settle the case, or you may be dragged before the judge, and the judge hand you over to the officer, and the officer throw you in prison.*
> Luke 12:57–58

In this scriptural passage, Jesus suggests that we make every effort to settle disputes, quarrels, and controversies before it is too late. He does not promise, however, that our efforts will always be rewarded with harmony and reconciliation. In my situation with my new boss, the effort I made to settle past accounts did not bring about a relationship based on mutual respect, but the Lord did provide me with his peace, which comes from choosing to obey his Word.

Judging Is Not Up to Us

Have you ever noticed how often we make snap judgments about people we hardly know? We catch a glimpse of a person and suddenly feel able to judge them by the words they speak, clothes they wear, and company they keep. Most often, if we can take time to get to know that person, we realize that our first impressions are, at best, superficial; at worst, dead wrong. As a Russian proverb says, "When you meet a man, you judge him by his clothes; when you leave, you judge him by his heart."

Judge No One

Perhaps it is human nature to judge. Most people have at least a small core of insecurity that comes out in the need to compare. Is she smarter? Am I richer? Is my school better?

More insidious is our need to judge the heart and soul of another person. "She's only doing this to get ahead." "He's a stingy person." "She wouldn't offer help if it would save her life." "He's not a very ethical person." "I wouldn't trust him farther than I could throw him." "Have you ever met somebody so irresponsible?"

You judge by human standards; I judge no one. Yet even if I do judge, my judgment is valid; for

> *it is not I alone who judge, but I and
> the Father who sent me.*
> John 8:15–16

Jesus cuts to the chase on our need to stand in judgment of others. "You judge by human standards; I judge no one. Yet even if I do judge, my judgment is valid." In other words, our limited human experience does not give us the perspective or right to pass judgment on others. If judgment needs to happen, we can be sure that God will take care of it.

Look for the Good

The next time you feel self-righteous judgment welling up inside you, try to catch yourself and analyze where the need to judge is coming from. Are you threatened by the other person? Are you feeling insecure about some aspect of your life? Do you need to stand out in the crowd? As the old adage says, "When you point a finger at somebody else, three fingers point back at you." Our need to judge usually says more about us than about the person we're judging.

*For some reason, we tend to evaluate other
people. Are they good or bad? Stupid or smart?
Rich or poor? Yet it's not our job to judge others.
That remains the work of God. Our job is
to love and accept others.*

When you feel the need to judge someone else, how about stopping to list five good qualities you notice about that person? If you can see their positive attributes, what you perceive as negative may not seem as important.

God calls us to love each other. This means being tolerant and accepting instead of intolerant and judgmental. Fortunately for us, God's spirit in us can help us make the leap from a negative thought to a positive thought. We can leave the complex job of judging to the One with a better perspective, and we can focus on loving acceptance.

* * *

Merciful God,

You love all of your children. You see the good in us all, and you help us grow to our full potential. Help me feel your love for me so that, when I am tempted to judge another person, I can remember we are equal in your sight. Give me a heart so full of love and acceptance that I have no need to be judgmental. Let me live in the spirit and name of Jesus Christ.

Amen

* * *

A Different Approach

We know just how it should have been done. If we were God, we would not have done anything like this—it would be a much different and certainly better world.

We would have set clear rules. We would have said, "Obey these rules and salvation is yours; disobey and you will be judged accordingly." We would have established a list of 101 commandments. We would have established an action-centered, law-oriented, sin-conscious morality, with every word, thought, and action clearly designated as right or wrong.

> *If you are pleased at finding faults, you are displeased at finding perfections.*
> Johann Kaspar Lavater

And when people missed the point of why they were created—to obey us—they would have suffered. Judgment and punishment—that's how to get people's attention and teach them to behave. If those human beings were foolish enough to persist in their perverse ways, we could wipe them out of existence. In fact, we might have avoided the frustrating situation entirely and never created humanity in the first place. One of the last things we would ever have considered doing was becoming human! Only someone much more loving than us would ever have done that.

There really is a difference between our human nature and the nature of the divine. That difference is not restricted to the limitations of our talents and powers, but it includes the varying ways we look at life and people.

Thankfully, we are not God. Our God does not give us lengthy lists of laws, but rather fills holy pages with stories and parables that tell how God's mercy and love exceed human understanding. God does not focus on what we are doing but on the kind of persons we are becoming.

And when we have sinned, when we have disobeyed, does God cut us off? No! God forgives us, welcoming us back with open arms. God wants our fellowship, and to convince us of this expansive divine love, God even came to earth as one of us.

I do not judge anyone who hears my words and does not keep them, for I came not to judge the world, but to save the world.
John 12:47

Our all-powerful Creator seeks not enforced obedience from us, but a relationship with us. For to be human is to be in relationships, and we are to be fully human. God has given us a will to choose and then hopes for our freely given love. How incredible!

There is a giant chasm separating human judgment and divine judgment, and that chasm is filled with love. God comes to us, cares about us—whether we consider ourselves worthy or not. The judgment we fear is a human-framed judgment made according to human standards. But it is God, in the person of Jesus, who says, "I came not to judge the world, but to save the world."

Jesus Urges Reconciliation

One Sunday, when my daughter was very young, she did something that resulted in a time-out for her and anger in me. I went to another part of the house to get ready for a trip to church. I was stewing about having to redo what I had already done when I heard the sound of little feet on the wooden floor. Her time-out was not over, but there she was, with teary eyes, wanting to reconnect with her father. She sought me out and helped me see the strength of our desire for reconciliation. We embraced, and I carry that valuable parable of reconciliation with me.

Be Reconciled First

When you are offering your gift at the altar,
if you remember that your brother or sister has
something against you, leave your gift there before
the altar and go; first be reconciled to your brother
or sister, and then come and offer your gift.
Matthew 5:23–24

Worship was a sacred duty in the time of Jesus.
For a Jew to be in a restored relationship with
God, the appropriate sacrifice to God had to be
made. Yet, as important as that relationship with
God is, if you come to the altar while there is still
enmity between you and another, Jesus advises
that you should first go and be reconciled. Jesus is
not overly concerned with who started the quar-
rel or disagreement, only that reconciliation is an
obligation for people of faith.

It doesn't matter who started the disagreement;
Jesus says seeking reconciliation is more important
than your obligation to worship.

I remember incidents in our neighborhood when
tempers would get heated in a teenage basketball
game and an adult would step in and tell us, "Say
you are sorry and shake hands." I never felt like
doing that, and often there would be a protest
that it was the other person's fault. Yet the adult
usually prevailed, and something happened in that
handshake that eased the confrontation. You cannot hit someone if you are holding their hand. The
basketball game would then go on, and I would be
amazed at the gift of reconciliation.

The Ministry of Reconciliation

As we grow older, we shift from needing adults
to guide us in reconciliation to adopting that

ministry ourselves. Paul says, "So if anyone is in Christ, there is a new creation: everything old has passed away; see, everything has become new! All this is from God, who reconciled us to himself through Christ, and has given us the ministry of reconciliation" (2 Corinthians 5:17–18). Now I am the adult teaching kids how to be reconciled when they disagree, and I still seek to resolve my own differences before going to worship.

The Church can model reconciliation and practice reconciliation. In our society, we are overly prone to get a lawyer. Many believe that nothing can be resolved except through the courts. We need to reestablish the practices of talking to one another, trusting God to lead us to reconciliation, and developing skills in the Church to resolve conflicts. The Church can be a leader in teaching the art of negotiation, the blessings of listening, and the skills of conflict resolution.

The next time you receive communion, be conscious of someone you would want to take with you to the Lord's table. Let that be the beginning of restoring relationships.

✳   ✳   ✳

God of mercy,

You invite us into the ministry of reconciliation. Give us the courage to take the first step, to seek out others, to listen to them, and to trust that you are present and working your will for reconciliation.

Amen

*　　*　　*

Clean Your Own House First

It's much easier to focus on the lives of other people than to honestly appraise who we are and what we do. Jesus encourages us to get our own house in order before we start making judgments about other people.

The Faults of Others

I don't know about you, but I find my own faults much easier to understand than the faults of others. There are certain characteristics, qualities, and actions that in myself I hope are endearing, but when I encounter those same traits in others, I find myself annoyed.

Why is it that most of us can easily see the wrong that others do but are less perceptive when it comes to realistically looking at our own lives? When I make a mistake, I may have an explanation of why it happened. I was tired, I rationalize. Or, I didn't get enough help from other people. I made a mistake because I needed support. I wasn't given all the information.

> *Instead of talking about other people's affairs,*
> *let me drive off my own wasps.*
> Japanese proverb

Because I see and understand things from my own perspective, my mistake may seem less important than someone else's error. Unable or unwilling to delve into another's experience, I judge them on what I see on the surface. Why did she mess up? There is no excuse! I can't believe he did that! I would never stoop so low.

Ah, but Jesus knows our game, even though these thoughts may never be spoken out loud. As usual, Jesus understands our humanness but seeks to lift us to a higher level.

The Log in My Eye

> *Why do you see the speck in your neighbor's eye,*
> *but do not notice the log in your own eye? Or*
> *how can you say to your neighbor, "Let me take*
> *the speck out of your eye," while the log is in your*
> *own eye? You hypocrite, first take the log out of*
> *your own eye, and then you will see clearly to*
> *take the speck out of your neighbor's eye.*
> Matthew 7:3–5

When we hear Jesus' words, we have to smile. We recognize that as easy as it is to see what's wrong with another person, it is harder to recognize and admit our own mistakes. Better (but harder) to take care of our own log before we worry so much about our neighbor's speck of dust.

Most people are like the Labrador spar crystal, which appears dull and ordinary until turned around and viewed at a different angle. When the light strikes it just so, the Labrador spar crystal sparkles with brilliance. So it is with other people; we need to look at them from a variety of angles before we can see who they are and why they do what they do.

To find a fault is easy; to do better may be difficult.
Plutarch

Etty Hillesum was a young Jewish woman who lived in Amsterdam at the time of the Second World War. Her journals not only show what it was like for a Dutch Jew in those dark times, but they also let us share in her spiritual struggles. In *An Interrupted Life: The Diaries of Etty Hillesum*, she reminds us of our need to take an honest look at ourselves: "There is a really deep well inside me. And in it dwells God. Sometimes I am there too. But more often stones and grit block the well, and God is buried beneath. Then [God] must be dug out again."

Taking the "log" out of our own eye is the process of digging out God when the stones and grit of our thoughts, words, and actions get in the way of our relationship with the Holy One. We may not be ready to tell other people about the ways we "fall short of the glory of God," but until we openly converse with our Creator about our real lives, the well is clogged, the log still stuck.

Seeking God's Help

Confession creates a renewed relationship with God in which we see that we don't need to focus on other people's faults, but rather we should take a close look at ourselves. Most of us would do well to start the day with quiet time in which we take stock of the previous day and prepare ourselves to accept the new day as a present from God and live it well.

Here are some questions we might use in such a meditation: Was the spirit of Jesus evident in the way I lived yesterday? Do I regret any of my thoughts, words, or actions? Are there people with whom I need to make amends? Am I open to how God might use me today in his work? How can I live in harmony with all people this day? What special help do I need from God in the activities I have planned today?

What You Give Is What You Get

One might say that "What you see is what you get" is a trademark saying of this generation. It sounds good, maybe even wise, to promote the concept of transparency in relationships. Yet looking at someone's personality and character, as important as that may be, is still only dealing with a limited dimension of life.

The Implications of the Golden Rule

Jesus was the source of another saying, the Golden Rule, which is far more relevant to our lives. Nevertheless, Jesus did not intend for the Golden Rule to be construed in terms of vague generalities.

For example, Jesus draws out what is involved with condemnation and forgiveness. It is simple enough to say that if you don't condemn, you won't be condemned. The same goes for saying that if you forgive, you will be forgiven.

Do not condemn, and you will not be condemned. Forgive, and you will be forgiven; give, and it will be given to you. A good measure, pressed down, shaken together, running over, will be put into your lap; for the measure you give will be the measure you get back.
Luke 6:37–38

Turn Jesus' sayings around, however, and you get an emotional baseball bat between the eyes! It's enough to make you break out in a cold sweat to think that if you condemn, you will also be condemned, or that if you don't forgive, you will not be forgiven. But that's the point. Thinking through what Jesus is saying is an exercise in wisdom. It will give you pause before you choose to condemn someone or refuse to forgive a person who has wronged you.

Like a Spiritual Pendulum

Nor does Jesus stop there in working out the practical implications of the Golden Rule. He advises his hearers to give, that it may be given back to them. At first glance, the Golden Rule and these initial explanatory points, especially this one, may seem like a reciprocation principle. That is, it all seems to work like a spiritual pendulum: You give (it swings one way), you get (it swings back your way), and back and forth the same way every time.

The Golden Rule, to "do unto others as you would have others do unto you," is almost universally recognized. But the Golden Rule is worded quite generally. What are some of its more specific implications?

In a general sense that is true, though our motive in giving should never be to get something back. Rather, the point is to assure you that the Lord will not let you become impoverished by virtue of how much you give.

But there is another assurance. The phrase "a good measure, pressed down, shaken together, running over" is straight out of the marketplace of Jesus' day. A true full measure was pressed down, shaken, and filled to the brim. If that was not done, one might end up being shortchanged. In other words, Jesus' wording here is an elaborate description of getting your money's worth.

Obviously, this description speaks of going to significant length. That reflects the lengths God will go to in making sure your giving to others will be responded to in full measure.

God Is in Control

Now that does not necessarily mean that the response will be "put into your lap" just as soon as you give to someone else. In fact, there is no promise anywhere in the Bible that you will be able to clearly discern when or how the full measure will be given back.

This wisdom relates to God's supernatural control over his created order. From a natural perspective, you give and it is gone. This is why people seek tax breaks, favors in return, and the like. Otherwise, they usually feel that giving is pouring resources down the drain.

From the supernatural perspective of Jesus' words, however, you give, God uses it, and then

God returns it, somehow, in full measure. Thus, giving is anything but a waste. It is a wise spiritual and eternal "investment," since you can be sure that the Lord is managing your portfolio with care.

*　　*　　*

Dear Lord,

I thank you for the assurance that you not only forgive, but that you also give back in the measure we give, often graciously even more.

Amen

*　　*　　*

An Old Time-Saver

These are busy days; we are all looking for ways to save time or energy. One time-saver that is as ancient as humanity itself is prejudice.

Prejudice saves us time, since we don't have to investigate opinions, develop new friendships, or visit places or events. Prejudice eliminates the effort we might otherwise spend in mind-stretching learning, in acquiring innovative ways of looking at the world's problems, or in understanding creative solutions to those problems.

How do we make decisions about people, about events and beliefs, about our priorities, even about ourselves? Making the right decisions can be quite a task.

The time that prejudice saves can be significant.
We can differentiate according to nationality
or skin color, gender or age or size, religion or
sexual orientation, school or workplace or resi-
dence, job or profession, dress or uniform or hair-
style, language or accent, size of family—there
are many ways to use the prejudice time-saver.
We need only be creative.

Placing every person, event, thought, or belief
into a box, labeled and categorized, reduces the
demands on our time. We can retain our same
opinions throughout life and avoid messy transi-
tions or the need to change our position.

> *Do not judge by appearances,*
> *but judge with right judgment.*
> John 7:24

Of course, every efficiency device, including
prejudice, does have a cost. As we use this time-
saver, we bypass opportunities to learn and to
develop interesting friends. Also, integrity and
truth are part of the personal cost. The world
loses the gifts and talents of those who are the
casualties of prejudice. And since prejudice is
easily transmitted, the world moves that much
further away from the possibility of peace, for
God's inclusive, radical, all-encompassing love is
again refused.

No Room for Throwing Stones

The word *hypocrite* comes from the Greek dramatic tradition of Jesus' era. It spoke of an actor who played a role and wore a mask that obscured his own features. The idea of "saying one thing and being another" is usually attached to hypocrisy today.

The group that Jesus continually labeled as hypocritical was that of the Jewish religious leaders, notably the self-righteous Pharisees. He used strong descriptions of them, calling them "whitewashed tombs," meaning attractive to the eye but dead on the inside.

Certainly there was no love lost between Jesus and these pompous leaders. He detested the total inconsistency between their religious image and their actual motives and behavior. They resented Jesus' appeal to the people, and they did everything they could to trick Jesus into some kind of mistake through which they could finally get rid of him.

None Are Without Sin

When they kept on questioning him, he straightened up and said to them, "Let anyone among you who is without sin be the first to throw a stone at her." And once again he bent down and wrote on the

ground. When they heard it, they went away, one by one, beginning with the elders; and Jesus was left alone with the woman standing before him. Jesus straightened up and said to her, "Woman, where are they? Has no one condemned you?"
John 8:7–10

This early morning encounter in the temple area was an unseemly attempt to force Jesus to be cruel or stand in opposition to the Mosaic law. Furthermore, nothing is said about how this woman was caught in her adultery. It has all the earmarks of a setup, however, especially since there is no mention of the man she was caught with, who was equally guilty.

The hypocritical religious leaders, the Pharisees, were testing Jesus, trying to force him to make a pronouncement opposing what the Law of Moses said about stoning adulterers. At the very least, they wanted to make him look like a fool. But Jesus expertly turned the tables on them. The hypocrites ended up with egg all over their faces.

"People who live in glass houses should not throw stones," advises the humorous saying. Since almost everyone has significant shortcomings somewhere in their lives, however, shouldn't we all let go of the rocks in our hands?

How did he do it? Jesus turned the spotlight from the accused to the accusers. He refused to focus on whether, morally, the woman should be stoned, but rather he focused on who was morally fit to do the stoning. Rather than stepping onto the trap-door that had been set up for him, Jesus pulled the rug out from under the hypocrites who were conspiring against him.

Jesus' brilliant statement was much of what turned this difficult confrontation around. Since there was no denying that everyone in the crowd (except Jesus) had sinned, even the consciences of the hypocrites were convicted, and they had to back off from acting as if they were morally superior.

From Humility to Compassion

Yet it appears that Jesus writing something on the ground also played a key role in all this. It is doubtful that Jesus was simply doodling in the dirt or merely playing mind games with the religious leaders.

There is no way to know for sure what he was writing. One plausible theory is that, when Jesus bent down, he was writing out the Ten Commandments in the dirt. Certainly the command "You shall not commit adultery" was the one at issue when the woman was brought before Jesus. Yet, other commandments, such as "You shall not bear false witness against your neighbor," also came into play, especially if catching this woman on this day was a setup. Whatever the case, the combination of Jesus' actions unnerved the accusers.

The wisdom of Jesus here relates to humility. None of us is in a position to be haughty in judging the actions of other people. That is not to say that there are not moral standards that must be guarded carefully if a society is to remain strong. It is to say, however, that no one except Jesus is in a position to make himself or herself the standard. Very often, compassion is the better part of wisdom.

*　　*　　*

Dear Lord,

Because I consistently blow it, I have to admit that I am in no position to condemn anyone else. Help me not be hypocritical but instead be gracious to those who fall short, as I have often done.

Amen

*　　*　　*

When Jesus Asks You to Be Merciful

*Blessed be the God and Father of our
Lord Jesus Christ, the Father of mercies and the
God of all consolation, who consoles us in all our
affliction, so that we may be able to console those
who are in any affliction with the consolation with
which we ourselves are consoled by God.*
2 Corinthians 1:3–4

The Quality of Mercy

Mercy is the capacity to understand the feelings of someone who is hurting, despite that person's culpability in the circumstances. In the film based on the book *Dead Man Walking*, the character of Sister Helen Prejean demonstrates the quality of mercy in many ways. The focus is on her relationship with a prison inmate convicted of rape and murder. It is a journey in search of redemption built on an admission of guilt, repentance, forgiveness, and mercy.

*If mercy is the ability to have compassion and
spare a person the consequences due him or her,
then mercy is rare. Today, people seem more
concerned with demanding justice than with
mastering the Christlike quality of mercy.*

In his last days before execution, the convict shows no remorse, insisting he is a victim and attributing his crime to bad influences and substance abuse. But Sister Helen cares as much about saving the man's soul as saving his life. When he attempts to affix blame on everyone but himself, she insists that he admit his guilt and begin to feel regret. At the same time, she does everything in her power to extend mercy to the man, his family, and his victims' families. When she is unable to get the man's sentence changed to life imprisonment, she offers to stay with him through his execution.

The quality of mercy is not strain'd;
It droppeth as the gentle rain from heaven
Upon the place beneath: it is twice bless'd;
It blesseth him that gives and him that takes.
William Shakespeare, *The Merchant of Venice*

At the end, the convict experiences God's mercy and forgiveness when Sister Helen refers to him as a "son of God," and he can look at her "face of love" as he enters death.

Blessed are the merciful, for they will receive mercy.
Matthew 5:7

The merciful extend mercy to others, thus extending God's mercy to them. When we offer the "face of love" to one undeserving of mercy, have we not become Christlike? As we season justice with mercy, we help others experience this part of God's character. In turn, we receive God's mercy and blessing.

The Vision of Peace

What is peace? Often, the peaceful reign of God is portrayed as an idyllic pastoral scene where people are engaged in endless repose. While occasionally we yearn for just such a calm existence, such a scene also prompts suspicions of boredom.

The Hebrew word shalom *is used today as a greeting in the Holy Land, just as we might use "hello" or "good-bye."* Shalom, *although often translated as "peace," conveys much more than that. It is a vision, a promise, a prayer for health and healing and wholeness, for community, for freedom, and for justice.*

Of course, God's peace is far richer than that. Picture it as the real presence of God's love throughout the universe. Peace is not just calmness; it is a vibrant commingling of our humanity, talents, and gifts. It is the reflection of the Spirit within each of us. Peace is unity glorying in our diversity.

We often think of peace as a lack of disagreement. More specifically, it is the harmonious settlement of disagreements. When we respond to the struggles of others, offering them hope or a solution to their conflicts, we are working toward a far more encompassing peace than we may think.

Peace will come to us only when we study what it is, pray for its presence, and work together to make it happen. The Bible calls us to be effective peacemakers. And while envisioning peace in today's world is difficult, if we do not make the effort to bring about peace, it will be that much more difficult for it to occur.

Most of us believe that "charity begins at home." We hope that by doing good among our own, goodness will spread out like concentric rings on the surface of a lake. And, if people pass their blessings along, that is true. Just for a moment, though, think of the water image in reverse. Say you start from far outside your home and the circles travel inward to the core. Wouldn't that encourage you to also act more globally?

Blessed are the peacemakers, for they will be called children of God.
Matthew 5:9

Our Mercy Comes from God

Because of their work hiding Jewish refugees, Corrie and Betsy ten Boom spent years in Ravensbruk, a Nazi concentration camp. Betsy eventually died there. After her release from the camp, Corrie ten Boom traveled around the world preaching a message of God's forgiveness. The strength of her belief was tested, however, when she met one of her former SS jailers at a Munich church where she had just preached.

God is our model of unconditional love and mercy. That means our love must also be specific to everyone we meet. Even if we find it hard to love, God's love and mercy can flow through us to others.

The sight of the jailer awakened ten Boom's painful memories of the camp. When he came forward to shake her hand, she was stunned to hear him say that Jesus had also died for his sins. Corrie ten Boom was unable to lift her hand to meet his. She couldn't even manage a smile. So she prayed for Jesus to forgive her and for help to forgive the man. She was still unable to respond. When she told the Lord that she could not forgive him, and she asked only for forgiveness for herself, she felt a current of love shoot down her arm toward the man she had every reason to hate.

There may be times in our lives when we need God's love and mercy to take over when our own fail. The good news is that not only did God show us how to love, but God's love is also available to us to share with others. As Saint Catherine of

Siena said, "The only thing we can offer to God of value is to give our love to people as unworthy of it as we are of God's love."

Those who look for reasons to
hate miss opportunities to love.
Carmen Sylva

Que Huong and her husband, Ngoc Phuong, lived quietly in their Vietnamese village until they found themselves caught between the opposing forces of their country's civil war. Not wanting to join either the revolutionary forces or the armies of the Thieu government, Huong and Phuong participated in a peace march for which they were arrested and thrown into prison. They were beaten and tortured, and finally, Phuong died.

When Que Huong was released from prison at the end of the war, she was asked what she would do if she met the man who had tortured her and Phuong in prison. The gentle woman replied that she still held the "flame of anger" inside her, but she knew that killing her torturer would cause his family to take revenge on her. She wanted the hatred to stop.

But love your enemies, do good, and lend,
expecting nothing in return. Your reward will
be great, and you will be children of the
Most High; for he is kind to the ungrateful

and the wicked. Be merciful, just as
your Father is merciful.
Luke 6:35–36

Throughout history, there have been persons who have shown love when hate would have been understandable. We are amazed when we see the ability to love even in the face of personal pain and loss, the capability to show mercy even when revenge would be a natural response. Can we be as forgiving? Does our mercy reach that far? We know that even though we try to live in love, at times we are angry, hurt, or eager for revenge.

Although he hates me, if I do not hate him,
enmity will soon be at an end.
Chinese proverb

Fortunately, God has given us the highest example of mercy: He sent his beloved Son, Jesus, for our sake. God enables us to begin each new day feeling loved and forgiven. And because we saw in Jesus one who could confront injustice without hating the unjust, we know that such love is possible—even for us.

But now in Christ Jesus you who once were
far off have been brought near by the blood of
Christ. For he is our peace; in his flesh he has
made both groups into one and has broken down
the dividing wall, that is, the hostility between us.
Ephesians 2:13–14

As Generous as Jesus

The Jesus of the Gospels was generous with his time. He sat with the woman at the well and led her to a new understanding of herself (John 4). He had time to hold children on his lap and bless them, despite the attempts of the disciples to move them along (Mark 10:13–16). He would interrupt his travels to respond to those in need of healing, as with blind Bartimaeus (Mark 10:46–52).

Jesus was generous, even with those whom others shunned. Jesus taught the crowd on the hill, using easily understood parables based on their daily lives (Matthew 5). In the midst of his Sabbath teaching in the synagogue, he touched and healed a woman who had been bent over for 18 years (Luke 13:10–13). Jesus was generous with his words and his miraculous touch.

The most generous gift we have ever received was Jesus Christ; through his example we are encouraged to find our own ways to be generous.

We usually think that generosity only involves money. Yet Jesus would prefer we show our generosity through service. A good way to practice generosity is by doing a private act of kindness or performing an unseen service. Practice giving that does not benefit you—we do not give in order to receive. Send a note of appreciation to someone who does not get much recognition. Do the dishes even if it isn't your turn. Pay for the car behind you at a tollbooth. Deliver a plant to a church secretary. Throw a surprise party for a friend.

In all this I have given you an example that by such work we must support the weak, remembering the words of the Lord Jesus, for he himself said, "It is more blessed to give than to receive."
Acts 20:35

Paul says that generosity is a fruit of the Spirit (Galatians 5:22). Generosity flows from the heart, from the abiding trust that God is at work. God is a God of abundance, and what we give away does not diminish us but clears out more room for God to be generous to us. The more we trust God in our giving, the more thankful our hearts become in seeing that everything is a gift from God. If we have freely received, then we may also freely give.

An old African proverb says, "It is the heart that gives, the hand that lets go." Pray that you might have a generous heart and enjoy finding all the ways you can give.

Not long ago, our church held a drive for families in another state that had been hit by devastating fires. Our community had also experienced fires, so there was a generous response. A couple of weeks later there was another fire, and a family from our church lost their home. They appeared in worship the next Sunday to thank the church for its support, to testify that they were going to survive, and to announce that the only things intact were those set aside for our campaign for the fire victims. They taught us about thankfulness and generosity that day.

> *Teach us, good Lord, to serve Thee as Thou deservest: To give and not to count the cost... To labour and not ask for any reward Save that of knowing that we do Thy will.*
> St. Ignatius of Loyola

The Balm of Forgiveness

For if you forgive others their trespasses, your heavenly Father will also forgive you; but if you do not forgive others, neither will your Father forgive your trespasses.
Matthew 6:14–15

Jesus is not implying that God's forgiveness for our sins is dependent on our forgiveness of others. Rather, he says that walking in fellowship with God is impossible when we refuse to forgive others. Our ability to forgive others can be broadened when we realize that we have been forgiven.

Unappreciated by Others

For 18 years my husband and I worked with junior and senior high students in a youth ministry program at a small church. In spite of a few occasional struggles over philosophy and budget, we always sensed the congregation's support and felt at home there. In the middle of our 18th year, we began to feel a sense of restlessness and a desire to rest or take a sabbatical. When we resigned from our positions, we felt confident that we would be deeply missed. Some reactions to our resignation, however, proved surprising—and painful.

Just prior to our departure, the church took a survey regarding ministries of the church. Some church members apparently felt that they should not pay us for our 30-plus hours a week since other ministry leaders "volunteered out of the goodness of their hearts." Some people wrote in questions such as: "Why is the youth budget so much larger than the children's ministry budget?" and "Why should the church focus so much effort and money on reaching out to students whose families aren't involved in our church?"

My heart was broken. After so many years of trying to help church members see the value of investing time, money, and ministry in the mission field on our doorstep, some of them still didn't get it. And then to question our integrity, our motives, and our stewardship—I didn't feel much like forgiving.

As we met for the last time with the congregation, we broached these issues and invited those who had problems with our ministry to discuss the topics. When no one came forward, the anger inside me began to build. This was not how I wanted to feel about our departure. How could I rid myself of anger and frustration when the persons who had written the remarks refused to step forward? My stomach was in knots, and I felt bitterness tightening its grasp on my soul.

Forgiven by God

Then it came to me. What a hypocrite I am! How can I ask God to forgive me for my shortcomings if I am not willing to forgive those who have hurt me? Clearly our critics at the church did not have the full picture of our ministry and were speaking from uninformed perspectives. They didn't know the level of our financial commitment, or that many students with whom we worked had no other Christian influence outside the youth ministry.

> *Forgiveness is the economy of the heart....*
> *Forgiveness saves expense of anger, the*
> *cost of hatred, the waste of spirits.*
> Hannah More, *Practical Piety*

Instead of complaining to God about these people, I needed to pray that God would make the emotional, spiritual, physical, and financial needs of those students real in the hearts of our critics, that one or more volunteers would step up to fill our shoes in the youth programs, and that the church as a whole would consider students from unchurched homes a fertile mission field.

How difficult—but necessary—it is to surrender our grievances and grudges to God! Denying forgiveness to others is selfish and self-destructive. But when we release our bitterness before God, we will find balm, liberation, and forgiveness for others and for ourselves.

Why Forgive?

Our immediate response in the aftermath of injustice, cruelty, betrayal, neglect, or abuse is often refusal to forgive. The act is too recent. We are in shock. We cannot forgive.

For a time we must go over what was done, entering into the pain and gently embracing our shattered core. Carefully, fearfully, we assess the damage done to us. Eventually, we encounter the question of forgiveness. And though our feelings and beliefs concerning forgiveness are in the spiritual and emotional realm, we describe the situation using terms and metaphors from the physical realm. We talk of being wounded, of hurting, of breaking hearts, of seeking or desiring healing, of bearing scars. We describe each reminder of the act as a reopening of the wound.

As long as we deny forgiveness to others,
we deny ourselves healing. Each retelling of
an injury removes the delicate scar tissue slowly
forming over our pain, and our bleeding begins
again. Each remembrance renews the injury.

As time passes, we may come to the conclusion that those who injured us do not deserve forgiveness; there may even be an absence of sorrow or remorse on the part of those guilty. Yet forgiveness is not dependent upon an admission of either guilt or sorrow; nor does forgiveness always reduce the hurt or injustice committed.

We, the wounded, have become the ones who are bound and held hostage to our experiences. Only forgiveness can undo those ties binding us to the past. Only forgiveness frees us for the life that we cannot fully experience until we have released the hurting.

Then Peter came and said to him, "Lord, if another
member of the church sins against me, how often should
I forgive? As many as seven times?" Jesus said to him,
"Not seven times, but, I tell you, seventy-seven times."
Matthew 18:21–22

It may be that we cannot forgive from our own strength and mercy. It may be that the starting point of our forgiveness is to immerse ourselves in God's forgiveness. Within God's unlimited love is found the mercy we lack. When we allow that divine flood of mercy to wash over us, it can cleanse us from bitterness and thoughts of vengeance. And then, enveloped in God's boundless love, the river of God's mercy flows both to us and to those who have injured us. That is when our scars become victory badges.

Forgiveness Flows

A friend of mine rewrote the Lord's Prayer in contemporary verse. I don't know if he started from the original Greek, but his version touched me. He wrote, "Let forgiveness flow from each one, to each one, to each one." The first time I prayed that, the addition of the third phrase struck me. It was so true. Forgiveness should flow and keep on flowing from each one, to each one, to each one. There is a dynamic at work in forgiveness. It starts a chain reaction. As we let go of the sins against us, it releases others who are also bound by past hurts and wounds.

It starts with recognition of our own need for forgiveness. A harsh word, an intentional rejection, or a forgotten appointment are not only breaks in our relationships, but they also affect our relationship with God. Early Christians understood this. When Jesus invites us to pray that our sins be forgiven, it is a step toward making amends with those we have harmed or offended. The forgiveness of God releases an energy in us to make peace with others.

Forgiveness for our sins or for someone who has sinned against us releases God's power to flow to us and those around us. Forgiveness is a powerful expression of our merciful God.

At the end of World War II, 20,000 German war prisoners were marched through Russia toward their country. As they entered Moscow, people lined the streets to look and to jeer at the generals strutting with their heads high in an attitude of superiority. Next came the German soldiers, weary and worn, bandaged and hobbling, heads bent down. An elderly woman in the crowd pushed her way through the police cordon and ran toward a soldier with a crust of bread for the hungry enemy. It released something in the crowd, and soon others offered a drink or piece of food as the soldiers marched along. There was still anger, but there was a deeper sense of recognition that each German soldier was some mother's son. It was a step toward forgiveness. One woman's act created a new possibility, set loose a new wave of forgiveness and compassion.

In Jesus' day, any rabbi with a group of disciples would teach them a way to pray. We have been blessed with the Lord's Prayer, and we are encouraged to make forgiveness a part of our prayer and part of our life. Forgiveness opens a path, clears a blocked stream so that we may be fully alive and in harmony with others. As we forgive others, we can discover the courage to forgive ourselves.

Forgive us our sins, for we ourselves forgive everyone indebted to us.
Luke 11:4

Are you holding on to another person's error? Can you ask God for forgiveness for your errors and also for the errors of others? Are you willing to let go of the burden of anger and resentment, guilt and recrimination, and move into the freedom of God's forgiveness?

Once More with Feeling

Fred was an active member of his local church. On Sundays, his fellow members saw him as a jovial, outgoing man, always ready to lend a hand. So when he first asked for a loan from another member—"Just a few dollars to tide me over"— nothing was made of it. One loan led to another, however, until Fred owed money—lots of it—to many people in the church. Fred's compulsive gambling finally came out when his inability to pay back his loans led to one woman's own financial problems.

"I'm truly sorry," Fred announced to person after person as he explained his problem. Each lender understood, forgave him, and hoped he would overcome his problem. The pattern repeated, however, as Fred's addiction overcame his desire to begin again. As hard as it was, the church members continued to forgive and love Fred—though they finally realized that loaning him money was not the loving thing to do, since it enabled him to continue his destructive behavior.

All of us stumble and fall occasionally, even in our spiritual lives. Jesus reminds us that whenever we make mistakes, we can repent and begin again. On the other hand, we are also called to forgive others every time they offer repentance. Sometimes that's harder!

Instead, after the repentance and forgiveness scenario had played out many times, some members gathered with Fred to talk honestly about his gambling compulsion. "You need help, Fred. This is not something you can lick by yourself," one woman said. "Give it to God, Fred," another person suggested, "and join a 12-step group so that you have a support system to maintain a healthy way of being." The woman whose own finances were in jeopardy because of her loans to Fred took a deep breath, looked Fred in the eye, and said, "I will go with you to your first few meetings. I want to try to understand what your addiction is like."

Fred found a group for recovering gamblers where he heard many stories similar to his. He met people who struggled with addiction and who were occasionally overwhelmed by it, acted hurtfully toward others, repented, and asked for forgiveness. Not everyone had been as fortunate, however, to have a loving community who shared God's mercy.

This church community took Jesus' words seriously: "If the same person sins against you seven times a day, and turns back to you seven times and says, 'I repent,' you must forgive." With addiction, however, they realized that mercy and forgiveness also meant helping the addict toward wholeness. Their money didn't help Fred live as a person of God; their forgiveness and support did help usher him into a new period of his life.

Forgiveness, No Matter What!

Forgiveness, as a concept, is easy to understand. It means to grant pardon for an offense. It also usually includes releasing resentment against the person who committed the offense.

Easy to Understand, Hard to Do

As easy as the idea of forgiveness is to comprehend, however, it is anything but easy to do. It is true that if the offending act is relatively small, forgiveness may come more easily. But that is usually because there was also little offense taken.

Whenever there is much riding on the offense, the accompanying emotions of anger and resentment usually become dramatically harder to defuse. In addition, it is easy to convince yourself that what you feel is reasonable. It seems as if it is your inalienable right to hold on to the rage.

From the Cross Came Forgiveness

When they came to the place that is called The Skull, they crucified Jesus there with the criminals, one on his right and one on his left. Then Jesus said, "Father, forgive them; for they do not know what they are doing." And they cast lots to divide his clothing.
Luke 23:33–34

As Jesus died in excruciating pain on the cross, he had much reason to resent. The envious and paranoid religious leaders had stalked him at length, arrested him on a trumped-up charge, forced him to undergo the injustice of a "kangaroo court," and sentenced him to death. He was then brutally beaten before being made to carry his own cross to the hill where the death sentence would be carried out—in the company of two hardened criminals.

Truly, it was a horrible death! Crucifixion produced intense suffering. First, driving nails through the hands and feet attached the person's body to the cross. Besides the unending, searing pain of those wounds, the weight of the body pulled the limbs out of joint. That made it extremely difficult to breathe and caused the internal organs to collapse on each other. In the end, most died of asphyxiation.

Roman citizens did not usually experience this cruel and lingering form of death. Crucifixion was actually a symbol of the brute power of the ruling class over the masses.

Yes, Jesus had plenty to resent, if he chose to do so. But he did not. Rather, as he hung on that hideous cross, he was primarily concerned with exactly the opposite: forgiveness. He asked his heavenly Father to forgive the very people who had unjustly done this to him.

Remember, Forgive, and Then Forget

How do you know if you have forgiven? Many believe that you have not really forgiven until you have forgotten the offending act. If the incident repeatedly comes to mind, it is evidence that you have not fully forgiven. The error in this thinking, however, is that, in forgetting too soon, we will never learn from what happened.

"I can forgive, but I cannot forget," is only another way of saying, "I will not forgive." Forgiveness ought

to be like a canceled note—torn in two, and burned up, so that it can never be shown against one.
Henry Ward Beecher

Forgetting something that is painfully vivid requires an active "erasing" of the memory. Rarely does it happen through amnesia or brain damage. Forcing yourself to forget requires repressing or blocking the memory, and doing either is unhealthy.

If anything, true forgiveness requires remembering, at least until you've truly forgiven. You have to remember what happened in order to come to terms with your strong negative feelings. Forgiveness becomes the choice to release the powerful emotions involved. Don't be discouraged if that choice has to be made repeatedly before your emotions are laid to rest.

Forgive Despite Their Ignorance

It is important to remember one other thing related to forgiveness. From the cross, Jesus said, "Father, forgive them, for they do not know what they are doing." As hard as it may be to fathom, sometimes one person can be grievously hurt by someone else's actions or words without that other person knowing. At other times, as with Jesus, those involved know their actions are serious. Yet those who crucified Jesus had absolutely no idea how serious. They had executed Jesus, the

Son of God, who was completely innocent of any of the charges leveled against him.

Jesus' example is sound, even if our emotions don't agree. If he could forgive, given what was done to him, we must at least realize it is important to follow suit.

Put away from you all bitterness and wrath and anger and wrangling and slander, together with all malice, and be kind to one another, tenderhearted, forgiving one another, as God in Christ has forgiven you.
Ephesians 4:31–32

Forgiveness can be a long and bumpy process, but it is worth it. If you stubbornly refuse to forgive, it is not so much the person or persons you refuse to forgive who are hurt. You are being eaten up inside by the resentment you refuse to release. The person you should have forgiven likely has no clue what you are feeling. Thus, if you don't forgive, all your precious emotional energy is being wasted—just as if you had flushed it down the garbage disposal.

*　　*　　*

My Lord,

I have trouble forgiving. I secretly prefer to hang on to resentment. Help me make the choice to forgive, even if it has to be made repeatedly.

Amen

*　　*　　*

Mercy Matters More Than Appearances

Apparently, behaving "for the sake of appearances" is as ancient as the time of Jesus. The Pharisees, a group of religious leaders of Jesus' day, desperately wanted to look righteous in the eyes of the people. As a result, they could not understand why Jesus chose the opposite stance.

For the Sake of Appearances

When you do things for the sake of appearances, you strive to be at the right place, at the right time, with, of course, the right people. That means that the sole reason you make an appearance at certain events is often to look good.

Sadly, people have attended worship for the same reason throughout history. Whether it is the giving of a special sacrifice, some earmarked offering, a high-profile pledge, or simply attendance at a spotlighted service, some get involved primarily for the sake of appearance.

> *Go and learn what this means, "I desire mercy, not sacrifice." For I have come to call not the righteous but sinners.*
> Matthew 9:13

Such appearances may impress a great many people. They will think well of you. They may even admire you . . . or at least the "you" they think you are. Jesus, however, clearly had no tolerance for such hypocritical piety, particularly when shown during the worship of the heavenly Father.

For the Sake of Others

Then we have Jesus. He always seemed to be at the wrong place at the wrong time . . . usually with the wrong people—at least from the Pharisees' perspective. For example, the Jews despised tax collectors. They were more feared than the IRS is today. The Pharisees could not imagine why Jesus would be seen with such riffraff. What the Pharisees didn't consider, or think was important, was that the tax collectors were deeply conscious of their sins in Jesus' presence, and thus they became contrite and were drawn to God.

What the Pharisees also overlooked was Jesus' motivation. He did not minister to people based on their appearance—an idea that was totally foreign to them. His choices were made to actually do good. When quizzed about his relationship with such rabble, Jesus answered using a powerful analogy: "Doctors don't spend time with those who are well, but with those who are sick!"

"Going through the motions" means you are doing something that should be done, but your heart is not in it. Is it the action or the motivation that counts?

Of course, the Pharisees were spiritually sick too. They just didn't know it. They were religious, but they weren't really righteous—just self-righteous. They had the appearances and images down pat, but not the reality. They showed no mercy and, accordingly, received none in return.

The lesson here is that Jesus has mercy on those who acknowledge their shortcomings. We need his mercy far more than we need to be seen as righteous. And we need to be much more merciful to others, rather than remaining absorbed in our own needs.

*   *   *

Dear Lord,

Help me not focus on how I look on the outside but on how I really am on the inside. It is so easy to want people to admire my appearances. I forget that I only need your mercy and that I need to be merciful to others.

Amen

*   *   *

Tell Others About God's Mercy

Satisfied customers pass on their sense of appreciation through word of mouth. If we are willing to tell others about some relatively unimportant product, what about telling them about God's incredible mercy?

Dravecky's Pitch Has a Message

Dave Dravecky was a good major-league baseball player who is better known for how his baseball career ended. While pitching for the San Francisco Giants, Dravecky discovered that he had cancer in his left arm—his throwing arm.

What was amazing about Dave Dravecky was that, after surgery and extensive therapy, he was able to make a comeback and pitch again in the major leagues. The sad end to that gutsy comeback came when, during a widely watched telecast, there was a "pop" like a gunshot from Dravecky's throwing arm as he delivered a pitch.

The bone in the arm, weakened by cancer therapy, had snapped like a dry, slender branch. Dave Dravecky would never pitch again. In fact, additional surgery proved necessary, and they removed the entire arm and shoulder to make sure all the cancerous tissue was gone.

What has Dave Dravecky done since the dramatic end to his baseball career? To a large extent, he has been telling other people about God's grace and mercy. Dravecky's book about his experience and his many public and church speaking engagements begin with his baseball career and his bout with cancer, but they climax with his testimony about what the Lord has done in his life.

The Man Left Behind

As he was getting into the boat, the man who had been possessed by demons begged [Jesus] that he might be with him. But Jesus refused, and said to him, "Go home to your friends, and tell them how much the Lord has done for you, and what mercy he has shown you." And he went away and began to proclaim in the Decapolis how much Jesus had done for him.
Mark 5:18–20

There is a very real sense in which the man Jesus healed was like Dave Dravecky. Certainly, his healing was more dramatic than Dravecky's. Yet, like the baseball player, his notoriety gave him the opportunity to tell many people what had happened to him and how God had mercifully acted on his behalf.

How much are you like Dave Dravecky and the man Jesus healed? Consider this: In one way or another, we all owe a great deal to God's mercy in our lives.

*   *   *

Dear Lord,

Open my eyes to your mercy in my life. And please show me the situations in which I can share that appreciation with those who need your healing compassion.

Amen

*   *   *

When Jesus Asks You to Be Humble

*Whoever becomes humble like this child is
the greatest in the kingdom of heaven.*
Matthew 18:4

Realistic Humble Confidence

Fishing can be an exercise in frustration, especially if your ego is on the line. If you brag
about how many fish you will catch or about how
big the fish you catch will be, the trip can turn out
to be a meal of humble pie. It is different when
you fish for a living. The cocky and shortsighted
don't last as professional anglers. They can't take
the waiting and the humbling.

On the other hand, there is a special kind of confidence that effective fishers possess. Even though
they know that many factors impact fishing, they
also know that alertness, shrewdness, and perse-
verance usually pay off in the end. Over time, the
large catches will be made—though sometimes in
ways you don't expect.

The Call

*As he walked by the Sea of Galilee, he saw two
brothers, Simon, who is called Peter, and Andrew*

*his brother, casting a net into the sea—for they were
fishermen. And he said to them, "Follow me, and
I will make you fish for people." Immediately
they left their nets and followed him.*
Matthew 4:18–20

Several of Jesus' closest followers and friends,
including Simon Peter and his brother, Andrew,
were veteran fishermen. From long experience,
they understood the patience and humility it takes
to land fish. They did not comprehend, however,
how to land a person by telling them about Jesus.
They possessed neither the patience nor the
humble confidence needed to be effective in that
special task.

From the shore of Galilee, Jesus had watched
Peter and Andrew fish. He realized that fishing,
in many respects, is like witnessing about the
kingdom of God to other people. But his future
disciples didn't comprehend that similarity. While
they possessed the proper humble confidence for
fishing, they had no experience in telling others
about Jesus. They tended to be either fearful or
falsely confident. That seems to be why Jesus
worded his call to Peter and Andrew the way he
did. He knew that if he asked them to move from
all they had ever known to the unknown, any
parallels to fishing would make the call less frightening to them.

The Response

Fishing for people was indeed a perfect illustration for fishermen. Peter and Andrew were much more comfortable in dealing with fish than people. But things would change for the better. The same alert patience that made them successful fishermen also made them highly effective fishers of people.

> *When some people go fishing, they expect the fish to jump into the boat. When that doesn't happen, they give up quickly. What can you learn from impatient fishermen that is of eternal significance?*

As apostles, Peter and Andrew—plus the other professional fishermen James and John—saw thousands of people respond in faith as they shared their own faith in Jesus. They "reeled them in" with the same kind of humble, patient confidence with which they had fished the Sea of Galilee.

The rapid response of Simon and Andrew to Jesus' call reveals a great deal about how they felt about future success. They left with Jesus immediately, not because they hated fishing, but because they knew that fishing for people was the wise way to invest the humble confidence they had learned.

* * *

My Lord,

Help me develop the kind of healthy humility that is a basis for an effective spiritual life.

Amen

* * *

Bigger Starts Smaller... and Grows

Not everyone can work up the nerve to attend their tenth anniversary high school class reunion. But if you do, you will probably agree that there are two interesting trends: You will see the early faders and the late bloomers.

Early Faders

Early faders are the people who topped out in high school or shortly thereafter. They were the ones who were unusually physically mature for the high school years. Often they were very attractive and considered among the coolest kids in school. And, back then, you tended to think things would always be that way.

Time marches on, however, and time can make a world of difference with the early faders. Full heads of hair and muscular physiques can give way to baldness and potbellies. The most beautiful female faces and figures can fill out from childbirth or weight gain.

It may come as a shock that many of the beautiful people that you remember aren't beautiful anymore by that fateful tenth reunion. Not only that, but most of those you thought of as big and scary aren't big and scary, either. What happened?

You grew! They didn't get any smaller; you got bigger. That prepares you for the second trend, the late bloomers.

Late Bloomers

At the reunion, it may seem like there has been an invasion of people you have never met before. And, in a sense, that is true. Some of those you went to high school with had not physically and emotionally developed into the people they have now become. You may remember them as small, awkward, and unsure. Ten years and a major growth spurt later, they have a polish and a confidence that was not there before.

Again, the subconscious thought that "Things will always be this way" is proven wrong! How someone or something starts may not provide an accurate idea of how things will turn out.

Take Michael Jordan, for example. His NBA scoring titles and world championships with the Chicago Bulls cause us to forget his humble beginning as a basketball player. Long before he was an All-American at the University of North

Carolina or an NBA superstar, Jordan was cut from his high school basketball team.

Not making the basketball squad would be humiliating for anyone. It may seem ironic from this vantage point, but there was a time when it certainly appeared unlikely that Michael Jordan would become one of the greatest basketball players who ever lived.

> *Much of our society is committed to a "bigger is better" philosophy. But with the focus on bigger, we tend to forget that bigger usually started smaller. How do we get a balanced perspective on the beginning of bigness?*

Another classic example is the artist Grandma Moses. For what would be an entire career for most people, Grandma Moses worked embroidering on canvas. Then, in her mid-seventies, her hands became arthritic, and she was unable to hold her embroidery needles.

So, at age 86, from the memories of her childhood in the late 1800s, Grandma Moses began to paint. Despite never having an art lesson, within three years her work was included in a major show at the Museum of Modern Art in New York City. She continued this astounding, late-found painting career and earned worldwide acclaim until her death, when she was more than 100 years old.

So beware of basing wider expectations on humble, present-tense appearances. Things often turn out dramatically different than they start. There may end up being a lot more present than the seemingly limited potential you now see.

The Mustard Seed

He put before them another parable: "The kingdom of heaven is like a mustard seed that someone took and sowed in his field; it is the smallest of all the seeds, but when it has grown it is the greatest of shrubs and becomes a tree, so that the birds of the air come and make nests in its branches."

Matthew 13:31–32

Jesus made a startling point about the growth of the kingdom of heaven. Like a very small seed planted, unnoticed, in a field, the growth of God's kingdom on earth had a humble beginning with Jesus and a few followers. But that was not the end of the story; it was hardly the beginning.

That small seed in Jesus' story may not have been noticed for some time. But it soon made itself known as it began to grow. Eventually, it grew into a tree large enough for birds to nest in its branches.

Similarly, the kingdom of God (or kingdom of heaven, since Jesus used these terms interchangeably) has grown by leaps and bounds. From a spiritual standpoint, like the tree of Jesus' story, God's kingdom has become a safe place for generations of believers.

What is the wisdom of Jesus in this case? It is that no one should underestimate the growth of the kingdom of God. Whether in regard to the faith of an individual or the presence of the Church in a community, the initial growth of God's seed may be imperceptible at first, but its eventual growth will be surprisingly significant.

*   *   *

Dear Lord,

I want to be part of your kingdom and its growth. I ask that you take the tiny mustard seed of my faith and cause it to flourish and bless the lives of others.

Amen

*   *   *

Who's Looking?

I have come to the hermitage on retreat. In this small cabin, all my needs are met: I have food and water, light, warmth, toilet facilities, books, a comfortable bed, and a table and chair. Absent are the distractions of a telephone and television. Though isolated in a wooded environment, I can relax, knowing I am but a short distance from those on duty in the office. I have come here to spend time with God. Alone, in such a private place, how do I pray?

In Jesus' time, piety was appraised through prayer, fasting, and almsgiving or charity. It was possible to put on the mask of piety by praying fervently in public, carrying fasting to an extreme, or making great displays of generosity. While the artifice of such performances impressed others, the unanswered question concerned what good was done for the soul.

Do I spend hours on my knees, reading the formal prayers of others? Do I call aloud to God—and wait quietly for an answer? Do I sing, worshiping God with word and song and breath? Do I stand, arms raised heavenward, in a timeless posture of prayer? Do I walk in the woods, seeking God in creation? Do I dance, praising the Cosmic Dancer with my entire body? Do I talk to God as I would my closest friend?

Or do I lie on the bed, silently raising mind and heart to God? Or do I lie prone on the floor in absolute awe before my Creator? Or sit cross-legged on the floor in meditation?

Beware of practicing your piety before others in order to be seen by them; for then you have no reward from your Father in heaven.

Matthew 6:1

How does my piety express itself here, in this isolated space, where I am seen and heard by God alone? Should I pray differently here than in public? Does it make a difference? To others? To me? To God?

*   *   *

Mighty God,

Hear my prayers. Help me keep my prayers directed at you—not at people I'm trying to impress with my piety. Give me the courage to explore creative ways to speak to you. Thank you, God, for listening to me.

Amen

*   *   *

Practicing Hospitality

There are often many layers of meaning to a simple act. When Jesus welcomed a child, he was showing us a way of welcoming God. The simplest deeds of kindness and hospitality, such as welcoming a child, have deep meanings.

What We Can Learn from Children

Then he took a little child and put it among them; and taking it in his arms, he said to them, "Whoever welcomes one such child in my name welcomes me, and whoever welcomes me welcomes not me but the one who sent me."
Mark 9:36–37

Jesus' act has great importance in our society, where children are often ignored or neglected. In our fast-paced world, many do not have time or take time to play with children. We are too busy to squat down and listen to a child, especially if they are not our own. Children, however, have something to teach us.

I remember when a family with an autistic son began attending our church. One Sunday, at the start of the worship service, the son walked up the center aisle and blew out the candles on the altar. I was pleased that no one got upset at this strange action. A fourth-grade boy then got up to help me relight the candles. He said, "It is all right. It's my birthday, and he just blew out the candles early." I was touched by the wise, accepting comment from the boy and the gracious understanding of the congregation. When we listen to children, we will be surprised and blessed by their deeds and words.

Humble Hospitality

On another level, Jesus is teaching the disciples that hospitality is not just practiced for friends, but it is extended to all, even to the poor and forgotten. In Jesus' day and in ours, children have little influence. They can't advance our careers or create wealth. So Jesus is saying that hospitality is to be extended to those who are children: those without influence or wealth or power.

We are a fearful society, locking our cars, bolting our front doors, and avoiding the eyes of strangers. It is hard for us to have hospitable hearts when we live in fear. Can we create an open space in our hearts and in our homes where we can welcome others who may be different from us? Hospitality also involves laying aside our fears long enough to receive the gifts that others may bring. It is one of the richest biblical concepts.

> *With a humble heart and the Bible's*
> *encouragement, we can reach out to*
> *welcome strangers into our homes.*

In the Old Testament, Abraham welcomed three strangers with a special meal. They turned out to be messengers from God (Genesis 18:1–15). In the New Testament, when two travelers to Emmaus invited a stranger to spend the night, Jesus responded by breaking bread and revealing himself as the risen Christ (Luke 24:13–35). Scripture is full of stories of hospitality to remind us that when we welcome a stranger as a guest, we may be entertaining angels or Christ himself.

Such hospitality comes from an open heart that trusts that God is present in each encounter and is the host of every meeting. We will probably be a little wary of strangers in our sometimes violent world, but as we move toward hospitality, we will break down the walls that divide us and create a corner of God's new community of love.

Creating Time and Space

One sign of such hospitality is the existence of groups that encourage travelers to stay in homes when they visit foreign countries. For a number of years, our family has belonged to an organization called Servas. As members of Servas, we have received into our home people from all over the world. We enjoy an evening meal together, provide a place to rest, and share some of what is interesting about our area. With broken bread and sometimes broken English, we have learned about other countries, shared stories, and formed some lasting friendships. Our children correspond with people from Scotland to New Zealand.

Likewise, when we have traveled, we have stayed in people's homes and gotten to know a new place through the eyes of the people who live there. We have been blessed to visit people who have stayed in our home. The hospitality of sharing food, conversation, and a place to rest has created ties that cross economic and political boundaries.

Hospitality creates a free space where people can be themselves and reveal the gifts they have to share. You don't have to be part of any group to begin the practice of hospitality. You can begin by looking around and being present to those you meet. Begin by inviting someone to dinner, or for tea, or to a barbecue. It does require creating some empty space inside yourself so that you are not preoccupied with your own agenda, which prohibits good listening.

When we say yes to visitors from another country, or when we invite someone into our house, we are saying we will make time and space for the guest. Frequently I have to ask myself if I am open to receiving another, if I am willing to be affected by their presence. To be truly hospitable is to be fully present.

At Home with Ourselves

Jesus would also have us practice hospitality with ourselves. Can we be open to all the parts of our own personalities? There are commercial pressures that make us feel like less than the gifted people God made us to be. Can we practice hospitality toward the way we look? Our shyness? Our playfulness? Our worry? Can we welcome the child within us? Such hospitality is a way of being comfortable in our own house, our own skin. When we are at home with ourselves, we can more easily create a hospitable space for others.

A Life of Service

Each of us is called to a life of service. God's voice may sound in our own inner conversations, in encouraging a friend, in hearing a specific need, or in realizing that we have specific skills that could help other people. How is God calling you to serve?

"The Greatest Man Alive"

At the age of 30, Albert Schweitzer was a teacher, a preacher, a world-renowned organist, and a published author. When he read an article about people dying in French Equatorial Africa (now Gabon), he felt that God was speaking to him as he read. "And you, Albert, would you give up everything to become a doctor and go to Africa?" Schweitzer's call to service led him to six years of medical school, where he specialized in tropical diseases. His fiancée, Hélène Bresslau, spent those years training as a nurse so she could join his efforts in helping the people of Africa.

In 1911, the 38-year-old man and his wife went to Lambaréné, in French Equatorial Africa, where they established a hospital to treat people with malaria, leprosy, yellow fever, and other diseases. Schweitzer persevered in his commitment to the people of Lambaréné despite hardship, two world wars, and separation from his family. Because of his generous giving of himself, Albert Schweitzer received the Nobel Peace Prize in 1952. Albert Einstein called him "the greatest man alive."

> *I don't know what your destiny will be,*
> *but one thing I do know: the only ones among*
> *you who will be really happy are those who*
> *have sought and found how to serve.*
> Albert Schweitzer

Schweitzer's greatness came from his ability to humbly live the life of a servant. He gave up the security of his comfortable life in Europe because he knew he could make a difference in Africa. He understood the Jesus who washed his disciples' feet and set a mandatory example for them and for us to follow.

The Master's Humble Example of Service

> *He said to them, "Do you know what I have done to*
> *you? You call me Teacher and Lord—and you are*
> *right, for that is what I am. So if I, your Lord and*
> *Teacher, have washed your feet, you also ought to wash*
> *one another's feet. For I have set you an example,*
> *that you also should do as I have done to you."*
> John 13:12–15

We can only imagine the mixture of emotions the disciples felt when their Lord and teacher knelt before them to wash their feet. Peter was especially uncomfortable, protesting, "You will never

wash my feet." When Jesus responded, "Unless I
wash you, you have no share of me," Peter quickly
replied, "Lord, not my feet only but also my hands
and my head!"

As confusing as the reversal of roles in that epi-
sode may have been to Jesus' followers, it has become for Christians an important picture of who
we are: servants of God. We understand ourselves
to be like Christ when we offer ourselves to help
others, not counting the cost or asking, "How
will this look? Is this task worthy of my position?
What will I get out of it?"

Three Paths of Service

Since Jesus first made clear the call to disciple-
ship, countless of his followers have discovered
their own calling to servanthood. Linda and
Millard Fuller answered the call to serve when
they founded Habitat for Humanity in 1976. Habitat offers low-income families a chance to own
their own home through the efforts of volunteers
who build the dwellings with the homeowner.
Thousands of people around the world have
decent housing thanks to the efforts of Habitat for
Humanity. Millard and Linda Fuller and countless
Habitat volunteers found their way to serve.

Peace Pilgrim set out on foot on January 1, 1953.
She felt called by God to a life of spreading both

global and inner peace, and so she walked for 28 years until her death. During those many years, she walked until she found shelter, fasted until she was offered food, and carried with her only a comb, toothbrush, ballpoint pen, copies of her message about peace, and unanswered mail. Peace Pilgrim walked thousands of miles in all 50 states and Canada because she believed that if everyone had a sense of inner peace, there would no longer be any need for violence or war. Peace Pilgrim found her way to serve.

> *You ask me to give you a motto. Here it is: SERVICE. Let this word accompany each of you throughout your life. Let it be ever before you as you seek your way and your duty in the world. May it be recalled to your minds if ever you are tempted to forget it or set it aside. It will not always be a comfortable companion but it will always be a faithful one. And it will be able to lead you to happiness, no matter what the experiences of your lives are. Never have this word on your lips, but keep it in your hearts. And may it be a confidant that will teach you not only to do good but to do it simply and humbly.*
> Albert Schweitzer

When 11-year-old Trevor Farrell saw a news report on the homeless in Philadelphia, he took a blanket from his home and gave it to a homeless person on the city streets that very night. Trevor's concern for those who live on the streets led to Trevor's Campaign, involving many people who donate time, money, clothes, food, and warm blankets for the homeless. Eventually, Trevor's Place, a homeless shelter, was opened in Philadelphia. Trevor Farrell found his way to serve.

God's Call to Servanthood

Most Christians will find a variety of ways to serve God in their lifetimes. Some people are active in their own church congregation, working with young people or missions or the grieving. In addition, many followers of Christ serve the greater community or world. Jesus' call to serve brings many responses.

Each of us must discern for ourselves God's call to servanthood. Is your heart touched when you hear of a particular need or situation? Perhaps you could offer your time to work with children with cancer or abused animals. Do you want to make a difference globally? Why not link up with a world hunger organization or collect Bibles to send to other countries? Do you have certain skills that might be useful beyond your own profession and family? You might volunteer as treasurer for an environmental organization or offer your legal services to battered women. Do you wonder who in your own neighborhood could use your service? Maybe there's an older adult who needs weekly help buying and transporting groceries. Opportunities for service are endless. Something as simple as spending two hours a week teaching an adult to read could transform that person's life.

If our hearts are open and our spirits generous, serving as Jesus served will give us opportunity after opportunity to experience his love anew as we reach out to others in his name.

> *Do all the good you can, By all the means you can, In all the ways you can, In all the places you can, At all the times you can, To all the people you can, As long as ever you can.*
>
> John Wesley

Power Serving

To achieve true greatness, we do not have to misuse or abdicate the power that has been bestowed on us. Rather, we are to use the influence we have to serve God and others.

Once upon a time, an important ambassador traveled a long distance to visit a powerful king. He had heard that an alliance with this ruler could provide great benefits to his own country. The reputation of this king's wealth and power was widespread.

The Royal Servants

As the ambassador left his car at the front door of the king's magnificent palace, he called to the young man under the canopy. "Valet? Quick, take care of my car. I have important business to attend to with your king!" The young man replied with a snappy "Yes, sir" as he took the man's car keys.

As the ambassador entered the palace, he was greeted by a woman who explained that the king had prepared a luncheon in honor of his special guest. Her demeanor was pleasant, yet when she asked the ambassador to take a seat in the reception area, he asked, "Don't you have something that's a little more private for distinguished guests?" So she led him down the corridor to a large, elegant library.

While strolling around the palace grounds before the luncheon, the ambassador saw a groundskeeper trying to remove an old stump. The man was covered with dirt and grime and smelled of sweat. While he pulled and pushed with all his might, the stump wouldn't budge. When the ambassador saw the groundskeeper struggling, he immediately started to help him. But a voice inside him held him back, whispering, "Maintain your dignity, by all means. You don't want to soil this expensive suit."

An hour later, the ambassador was seated in a place of honor at the luncheon table. He heard the doors open and a voice that said, "I'm so glad you could join us." As he stood and turned to greet the king, he felt faint. For as he watched, in walked the valet, the receptionist, and the groundskeeper. But how different they looked! Each was wearing a handsome suit and a large gold ring with the royal crest. They took their seats directly across from him.

The groundskeeper spoke first. "I am the king of this land and these are my children. In fact, everyone in this kingdom is an adopted child with all the rights due a prince or princess." The ambassador finally gathered his wits enough to reply, "If you are all royalty, why did you try to trick me by acting like lower-level employees and servants?"

> *Jesus called them to him and said, "You know that the rulers of the Gentiles lord it over them, and their great ones are tyrants over them. It will not be so among you; but whoever wishes to be great among you must be your servant."*
> Matthew 20:25–26

The receptionist/princess answered, "We didn't try to trick you, sir. Everyone in this kingdom is committed to the life of a servant. We are truly royalty, but we serve willingly." "Yes," added the groundskeeper/king, "and all who would ally themselves with us must adopt our practices. Are you willing to join us?"

The ambassador could hardly believe he would be considered a son. His voice cracked as he answered, "Sir, I would love to stay here and learn your ways." "Good," said the king. "We start to-morrow." With a gesture from the king, the valet/prince handed a hanging bag to the ambassador. The king explained, "Here is your royal suit, your ring with my royal crest, your work boots, and ointment for the blisters that you will surely have by this time tomorrow. But perhaps with your help I can finish removing that stump."

Then they all commenced eating the sumptuous meal that had been prepared, and the ambassador never felt so much at home.

The Path to Servanthood

God guarantees all of us opportunities to serve when he indicates that it is not those who abuse their power who will achieve greatness. Instead, the path to becoming great in God's sight is through humbly serving others, a path that even children can follow.

Some of us have gotten the wrong idea about servanthood. We think that to be humble ser-vants we must abdicate our power and influence to others. For example, to be a servant to my employees, must I yield to their pressures for policies that would be unwise for the company? Does a servant attitude demand that I always put activities, committees, and meetings at church before my family's activities? Can I serve if I must also be a leader?

God has called us to be servants and to serve by leading. No greater example of this principle exists than Jesus himself. He did not come into the world to be served, but to serve and give his life as a ransom for us.

True service comes from a relationship with the divine Other deep inside. We serve out of whispered promptings, divine urgings. Energy is expended but it is not the frantic energy of the flesh.
Richard J. Foster, *Celebration of Discipline*

Jesus is the greatest leader who ever walked or served this earth. He served the people who followed him by meeting their physical, emotional, and spiritual needs. He served his disciples by teaching them the Word, telling them powerful stories, and empowering them to go out and share what they had learned with the world. He serves us today as our Savior, high priest, and advocate before God. His greatness is unmatched.

Neither selfish ambition nor resentful service will lead us to greatness. A servantlike attitude of humility must be genuine.

But what would happen if we allowed divine urgings to prompt us into service? What would happen if we decided to use our power and influence to serve our family, friends, coworkers, church, and community?

If we become like Jesus, our wishes for greatness will surely be granted.

Made in God's Image

Jesus came to turn our world upside down. He came to teach us to look at people and institutions and God through new lenses. He came to teach us, by his words and his actions, what our heavenly Father, and not humanity, considers the virtuous life.

Forced Humility

> *All who exalt themselves will be humbled, and*
> *all who humble themselves will be exalted.*
> Matthew 23:12

It is within this context of virtue that Jesus taught us the paradox of pride and humility—where the first shall be last and the last first. How contrary this is to human standards and judgment!

Since this has been difficult for us to accept, we have taken this paradox and often interpreted it for our own purposes. Throughout the history of

Christianity, humility has been misappropriated by the powerful and dominant to quell the rights of others by using the command, "Be humble!" It has been used by races and nationalities and classes and countries to keep others from enjoying freedom or recognizing their own worth or fulfilling their potentials.

Humility has been the excuse given by institutions to keep members from using their God-given gifts; it has been used by whites to justify keeping people of color in subjugation; it has been used by men to keep women in submission. It has been, and continues to be, called upon by individuals to keep others in a state of obedience.

None of these instances reflect Jesus' view of humility; none of these instances reflect God's inclusive radical love.

Equal Before God

It is easier to describe humility by stating what it is not. Humility is not self-abasement; it is not demeaning. And while honesty demands that we admit both our limitations and our sinfulness, we must also, in truth, recognize our blessed and gifted humanity. Regarding ourselves as worthless or denying our talents is insulting, even blasphemous, to our Creator, in whose image we have been created.

Neither is humility expressed in prideful self-importance or in placing ourselves above others. Love and truth demand the recognition of the dignity and equality of all people before God.

Humility is always in tension between these two extremes: admission of our flaws and recognition of our atoned humanity. Humility thrives in the balance.

Perhaps humility is more easily recognized by the company it keeps, for it is a virtue that never flourishes alone. Humility is joined by honesty, truthfulness, joy, integrity, a hunger for justice, honor, self-acceptance, love, sincerity, accountability, and, let us not forget, a sense of humor.

*　　*　　*

Thank you, God, for creating ME!
Truly I am wonderfully, marvelously made!
From your love and wisdom have I come
To this place and time.
To me you have given talent and life and blessings.
With joy and gratitude
I celebrate my much-honored existence.
From ages past to eternity,
I have been included in your divine plan.
Thank you, God, for creating ME!

*　　*　　*

When Jesus Asks You to Be Wise

[God] is the source of your life in Christ Jesus, who became for us wisdom from God.
1 Corinthians 1:30

Wisdom, a New Heart

He came to his hometown and began to teach the people in their synagogue, so that they were astounded and said, "Where did this man get this wisdom and these deeds of power?"
Matthew 13:54

The people of Nazareth had seen Jesus grow up. They knew his mother and father, his brothers and sisters. Matthew reports that they were astounded and then offended by his claims about himself. How could someone so ordinary be saying what Jesus said? He was judged by his background and his family. Yet, even though they hated to admit it, Jesus was an amazing teacher.

Centered on God

Jesus was a teacher of wisdom; his words and his life drew people into the presence of God. In Jesus, people could catch a glimpse of God. As a teacher of wisdom, he called and challenged people to center their lives on God, to trust that the maker of the universe was a gracious and compassionate God. His teaching went against the common wisdom of his day.

The wisdom of Jesus' day was concerned with personal identity and security. Wealth and possessions were not only a way to comfort and ease, but they were also thought to be signs that God looked upon you with favor. Jesus warned of the dangers of riches. "How hard it will be for those who have wealth to enter the kingdom of God!" (Mark 10:23). Though Jesus associated with the rich and had some wealthy supporters, it is clear that Jesus saw money as a distraction from living a godly life, and he saw that greed puts blinders on people so they can no longer feel compassion. Jesus presented an alternative wisdom, one that was centered on God and service to others.

A Loving God

In Jesus' day, even religion had become a means to identity and security. People wanted to be descendants of Abraham and live according to the rules. The Pharisees thought they were models of religious life because they faithfully adhered to the most rigorous standards of the day. Yet Jesus often criticized the Pharisees because their security was based on their own religious accomplishments. In contrast, Jesus lifted up the example of the tax collector who prayed, "God, be merciful to me, a sinner!" (Luke 18:13).

Jesus brought a wisdom that centered on the heart, the deepest center of a person. The religious externals were less important than the motivations. "Blessed are the pure in heart, for they will see God" (Matthew 5:8).

Jesus challenges the conventional wisdom with a new wisdom of the heart.

The wisdom of Jesus centered on God. A radical trust in God is contrasted with the anxiety of trying to make it on our own. Jesus invited his followers to let go of worry about food, possessions, and security. He asked them to surrender their lives to God. He invited his followers to see that at the heart of everything is a God who loves us. Therefore, we are to trust God.

Jesus' Invitation, Then and Now

For his friends in Nazareth, the invitation from Jesus was intriguing and frightening. They could see his wisdom, but they knew the security of possessions and of following the religious leaders. They had their families to think of and their careers to advance. Could they trust God to provide?

We wrestle today with the same invitation. Jesus asks us, "Where is your heart?" Do our activities flow from the center of God's grace and guidance?

*　　*　　*

Dear God,

Give me a new heart, one that is led by your wisdom and not the world's wisdom. Help me see that your bounty is more valuable than any wealth I could accumulate. Teach me to be pure in heart.

Amen

*　　*　　*

A Model for Balanced Growth

When a tire on your car is out of balance, the car does not run smoothly. If the tire is not worked on to bring it back into balance, it will wear out (or blow out!) much more quickly than the others.

This illustration can help us understand balanced living. Your life is like a tire because it must be balanced to flow smoothly. Like spokes on a wheel, there are at least four areas of life that need to be in balance: the intellectual, the physical, the spiritual, and the social. When the balance of these four is out of whack, life begins to get bumpy and may soon break down.

The Physical and Intellectual Growth of Jesus

Jesus is history's classic example of balanced growth. To be sure, as the Son of God, he was already perfect and no growth was required. But the humanity of Jesus was not just an illusion or a front. He was just as much human (despite never sinning) as he was divine. And, as a human being, he grew.

That growth is perceived most easily in the physical realm. Jesus was born to Mary and Joseph as a healthy human baby; then he went through all the normal stages of growth to adulthood. There is no indication that Jesus was in any way out of the ordinary during those years of physical growth.

> *Jesus increased in wisdom and in years,*
> *and in divine and human favor.*
> Luke 2:52

Jesus also grew in the intellectual sense. A stunning example of this took place when Jesus was 12 years old and went with Joseph and Mary to a feast in Jerusalem. He astounded the Jewish teachers in the temple with his grasp of Scripture. Yet, as much as he already understood, we are told Jesus still grew in wisdom.

The Spiritual and Social Growth of Jesus

Just as physical and intellectual growth are necessary for a balanced life, so are spiritual and social growth. They are, however, more difficult to get a handle on.

There is evidence that Jesus also grew in these last two areas. In the spiritual realm, he made prayer the highest priority. For example, Jesus prayed all night before he chose the 12 apostles. Then, in the Garden of Gethsemane, he struggled in prayer in order to finally accept the Father's will that he die on the cross.

When a person's thinking and actions become clearly irrational or delusional, that individual is considered unbalanced. Oddly, however, you rarely hear discussed what is meant by "balanced." Is there a clear model available that embodies such balance?

Socially, Jesus also built close relationships. He was very close to Mary, his mother. His closest friends were Peter, James, and John—the inner circle of the apostles. Beyond them, and the rest of the apostles, were other close male and female friends.

Since Jesus is God, perhaps growth in these areas was easier for him. Jesus was the perfect role model. We can live balanced lives by choosing to pursue intellectual, physical, spiritual, and social development every day.

*　　*　　*

My Lord,
I admit that my life is not as balanced as it should be. Grant me the wisdom to develop a life that is

well rounded in your eyes. Help me be increasingly like Jesus.

Amen

* * *

Putting Words in Your Mouth

The phrase "putting words in my mouth" is usually used when someone is complaining. It means they feel someone else is misrepresenting what they really want to say.

In effect, accusing someone of putting words in your mouth is accusing them of being a ventriloquist. You open your mouth, but the words that emerge are not really your own words. You can end up mouthing the wording provided by the other party.

Of course, few of us want to say what we don't mean, and particularly when what we say is contrary to our beliefs. That's one reason why religious persecution is so unnerving.

Under Fire

Under religious persecution, people are called upon and asked to defend their beliefs. They can face suffering, imprisonment, or even death if they don't respond as the persecutors want them to. The way persecutors treat their victims is calculated to terrify the people on trial. If the strategy is successful, the defendants may provide crucial information or even recant their beliefs.

One of life's biggest fears is that when we have to face a frightening event that requires an immediate response, we will simply freeze up and not know what to say or do. Wouldn't it be wonderful to know that the wisdom to handle the situation will be there when you need it?

Perhaps the biggest difficulty in attempting to survive this kind of trial is that one often faces such circumstances in isolation. As long as there is a support system, most people can withstand a great deal. But if you feel all alone, it is much harder to take the pressure.

You Are Not Alone

While persecution or other trials may seem to leave you all alone, you really are not alone. The Lord has promised, "I will never leave you or forsake you"; his spiritual presence is always present. Moreover, he has also made another incredible promise: He will, somehow, put the right words in your mouth, at the right time, in order for you to defend yourself.

This will give you an opportunity to testify. So make up your minds not to prepare your

> *defense in advance; for I will give you words*
> *and a wisdom that none of your opponents*
> *will be able to withstand or contradict.*
> Luke 21:13–15

Now, that does not mean that nonbelievers will always be satisfied with what you say. But it does mean that God's viewpoint will be presented powerfully enough to impact someone with an open mind.

History is full of examples of those who did not think they could speak up under such difficult circumstances. Then, when the time came, they heard their own voices speaking eloquent words that were at once their own, yet seemed to come from another source, a higher power.

Being placed on the firing line to defend your faith is not something that most people look forward to. Yet, if it were to happen, it is a great comfort to know that the Lord would provide the wisdom needed to respond properly, at just the right time.

*   *   *

Dear Lord,

The very thought of having to stand up and answer for my faith terrifies me. Thank you for promising to provide the wisdom I need, should I have to face such a challenge.

Amen

*   *   *

Like a Little Child

Do you remember Hans Christian Andersen's fairy tale "The Emperor's New Clothes"? The emperor heard that two weavers could make clothes that had the peculiarity of being invisible to anyone who was hopelessly stupid. Hoping to identify the clever statesmen from the stupid in his court, the emperor hired the weavers to design an elaborate new outfit for him to wear in a procession through the village.

All the emperor's officials, chamberlains, prime ministers, and gentlemen-in-waiting dared not let it be known that they couldn't see any clothes. Even the emperor was afraid to admit that he couldn't see anything. Thus the emperor proceeded through the town stark naked. But one small child in the crowds cried out, "But he hasn't got anything on." The whispering began and spread until people were shouting, "He hasn't got anything on!"

With that innocent observation, a small child revealed the truth about the emperor's invisible wardrobe.

Marie's Inspiring Faith

Children often exhibit simple wisdom. They catch us off guard by stating or doing the obvious when we adults are experiencing fear or embarrassment.

Take my friend Marie, a wonderfully perceptive seven-year-old girl who dreams of someday becoming a great archaeologist or missionary—or both! A highly imaginative child, Marie intuitively seems to know how to help others dream. As I listen to her sincere prayers before meals, it is clear that the Holy Spirit has softened her heart. I am struck by her sensitivity to the needs of her friends, family, neighbors, and even those hurting and in distress around the world.

During the winter months when the youth ministry group sponsored by her mom volunteered to serve meals to the homeless, Marie once asked if she could tag along. With her mom's permission, Marie dressed in her best pink leotard and tutu. Because she was too small to ladle soup or serve coffee, she offered all those gathered in the warm church an unusual gift—a ballet of her own creation.

The followers of Jesus were not the most important people of their nation. Nor were they considered the "wise" or "intelligent." Rather, God revealed his great mysteries to those who became like little children.

Like a little elf, Marie twirled and leaped, humming under her breath as her long blonde hair flowed behind her. An old man wrapped in a bulky tweed coat and a single mother with small children smiled as the animated little girl spun across the room with effortless grace. The folks huddled over their hot food, but they couldn't help watching the little blonde fairy as she darted around the room.

Even the members of the student ministry team stopped to watch the little ballerina entertain her audience. With the bleakness of the winter winds howling outside, Marie's wise, unselfish act of service was refreshing to the heart and not unlike King David's dance (see 2 Samuel 6:14). How like a little child to lead us in understanding the special, unseen needs of others!

Faith Like a Child

No matter how wise or smart we are, no matter how old we are, we will never be able to understand everything about heaven, humankind, or this galaxy in which we live. God has hidden the great mysteries of his wisdom from all of us, particularly from those of us who consider ourselves to be wise and educated. Instead, he chooses to whom he will reveal the truths of how we should live, and sometimes he does so through the simplest means, such as the words and actions of a little child like Marie.

> *At that time Jesus said, "I thank you, Father, Lord of heaven and earth, because you have hidden these things from the wise and the*

*intelligent and have revealed them to infants; yes,
Father, for such was your gracious will."*
Matthew 11:25–26

The one thing we can understand is that gaining
wisdom can only be experienced by those who
come to God in childlike faith. And as we become
like children—observant, intuitive, uninhibited,
sensitive, giving, caring, jubilant—he receives
us with joy and delights in us as he imparts his
wisdom.

*   *   *

Lord of all creation,

*When I read the words of Jesus, I know that true
wisdom resides in him. He has the insights to guide,
encourage, comfort, and strengthen me. He declares
the truths that reveal who I am without you and who
I can become when I am obedient to your will.*

*Thank you for the gift of Jesus and what he means to
me. And help me profit by his wisdom so I can live the
abundant life that you have promised your children
and, more important, so I can serve others humbly and
lovingly.*

Amen

*   *   *